— Commendation

" Given the grim choice- in November, some of us m~ ~~~ ~~~~~ ror president. That's a quixotic move, though, so the better alternative might be to teach the principles David thoughtfully expounds and persevere in the faith that in 2020 our vision will improve."

— **Marvin Olasky,** editor-in-chief at WORLD News Group and author of *The Tragedy of American Compassion*

" In *The Voting Christian*, David Innes provides a refreshingly accessible approach to Christian political thinking. Sound and sober, free of political cant, he tackles all of the hot-button issues. Written with a lively blend of political theory and common sense, Innes delivers what he promises: wisdom for the ballot box."

— **Joseph Loconte,** Ph.D., is an associate professor of history at The King's College in New York City and the author of *A Hobbit, a Wardrobe, and a Great War: How J.R.R. Tolkien and C.S. Lewis Rediscovered Faith, Friendship, and Heroism in the Cataclysm of 1914-1918*

" *The Voting Christian* is loaded with wisdom for every American Christian (and many Christians elsewhere) on basic principles and how they apply to the choices we face in the voting booth— not just in the coming Presidential election but in elections from most local to most national. David C. Innes of The King's College deserves widespread thanks for his service to sensible Christian thinking on principles, on issues, and on candidates."

— **E. Calvin Beisner, Ph.D.,** Founder and National Spokesman, The Cornwall Alliance for the Stewardship of Creation, and author of *Prosperity and Poverty: The Compassionate Use of Resources in a World of Scarcity*

" Few scholars combine the seriousness and care with which David C. Innes approaches and reflects on the relationship of faith and politics. At a time when politics appears to have been replaced with Kabuki Theater, conscientious and politically interested Christians will greatly appreciate this collection of essays addressing the theory and theological significance of what is unfolding around us."

— **Douglas Minson,** Senior Fellow at *The John Jay Institute*

THE ☑OTING CHRISTIAN

SEEKING WISDOM
FOR THE BALLOT BOX

D. C. INNES

GREAT CHRISTIAN BOOKS
LINDENHURST, NEW YORK

Great Christian Books
is an imprint of Rotolo Media
160 37th Street Lindenhurst, New York 11757
(631) 956-0998

Innes, David Colin, 1962 -
The Voting Christian / by D. C. Innes
p. cm.
A "A Great Christian Book" book
GREAT CHRISTIAN BOOKS an imprint of Rotolo Media
ISBN 978-1-61010-014-4
Recommended Dewey Decimal Classifications: 200, 230, 239
Suggested Subject Headings:
1. Religion—Christianity—Politics
2. Political Science—Christianity—Apologetics/Polemics
I. Title

Book and cover design are by www.michaelrotolo.com. This book is typeset in the Minion, Myriad and Trajan typefaces and is quality-manufactured on acid-free paper stock. To discuss the publication of your Christian manuscript or out-of-print book, contact us.

Manufactured in the United States of America

CONTENTS

Introduction

I was recently interviewed by a Brooklyn media outfit on how evangelicals see the current election. Several times I was asked, "So who is God's candidate?" I didn't give a straight answer because it's a complicated question. Nonetheless, it's one that Christians are required to ponder.

On one level, "God's candidate" means the one who intentionally and perfectly conforms his policies and judgments to the mind of God. But there is not, and cannot be, such a candidate. Only King Jesus fits that description. On another, quite unavoidable level, God's candidate is the one he will raise up by our democratic republican system to govern us. But that, of course, is his business. "The secret things belong to the Lord our God, but the things that are revealed belong to us and to our children forever, that we may do all the words of this law" (Deut. 29:29).

The question can also be asking, however, which of the candidates—given what God has revealed of himself—does God want us to select. In the past, that question has seemed deceptively easy to answer. I say deceptively easy because it is never as easy as we think it is, as though in a given contest no serious examination of the candidates were necessary and no careful investigation of Christian principles and sober anticipation of natural consequences were in order. And as though that itself were easy.

In 1976, the Southern Baptist Jimmy Carter seemed to be the evangelical choice. In 1980, his opponent, the Moral Majority backed Ronald Reagan seemed an equally clear choice, despite his divorce and irregular church attendance. Or perhaps just looking back it seems that way. In 2000, it seemed to be George W. Bush, the born again Reaganite. And yet today many conservative evangelicals are lamenting—this side of their humiliating defeat in the culture wars, from fighting the feminist ERA to defending the DOMA citadel—how those battles and devotion to those champions distorted the gospel not only in the public eye but even in their own understanding.

Yet the Christian is inescapably a citizen not only of Christ's heavenly kingdom but also of this earthly republic of laws. And by God's great mercy, government in America is not just something other people do in faraway places and impose on us, though sadly that is increasingly so. It is still the beauty of what Lincoln described at Gettysburg as "government of the people, by the people, and for the people."

If a Christian people is to govern itself and choose wisely those who will represent them in their decision-making responsibilities, then Christians need to be properly informed. They need godly wisdom. They certainly need to understand, as the Westminster Shorter Catechism says (Question 3), what the Scriptures principally teach, i.e., "what man is to believe concerning God, and what duty God requires of man." But the Book of Proverbs teaches us,

> I, wisdom, dwell with prudence.
>> And I find knowledge and discretion
> The fear of the Lord is hatred of evil.
> Pride and arrogance and the way of evil
>> and perverted speech I hate.
> I have counsel and sound wisdom;
>> I have insight; I have strength.

By me kings reign,
   and rulers decree what is just;
by me princes rule,
   and nobles, all who govern justly. (8:12-16)

Christians in their capacity as free citizens have a responsibility to seek and grow in civic wisdom. This wisdom fits them to participate helpfully in the tasks of self-government for the common good and the glory of God. Though this certainly begins in the fear of the Lord, it culminates in making wise and prudent judgments concerning difficult matters that confront us in a world clouded and twisted by sin. This wisdom requires us to clear our heads, inform our minds, and chasten our hearts for distinguishing Christ from the world and the love of God from infatuation with the world, the flesh, and the devil—the lust of the eye, the lust of the flesh, and the pride of life, as the old King James Version rendered the beloved disciple's warning (I John 2:16).

This book is far from sufficient for that task. Ideally it calls for a life's worth of learning in the Scriptures, the insights of those greater than I, and as complete a knowledge of current affairs as one can reasonably muster. But if the reader is urgently occupied with family, business, church, and community and needs a handy help for understanding the times, perhaps this book will do.

I wish to thank Marvin Olasky, the editor-in-chief at WORLD magazine, for giving me the opportunity to write a weekly online column for several years, and my editor there, Mickey McLean, who made me a better writer and restrained my overstepping on more than one occasion. This volume is a collection of those short essays which have been adapted in places for this particular purpose, and I thank WORLD News Group for their gracious permission to use them. I also thank Pastor Benjamin Miller and all the saints at Trinity Church (OPC) on Long Island, NY, and my colleagues and students at The King's College in Manhattan for their part in helping me to become a humbler and more thoughtful Christian.

—Section I—

PRINCIPLES

1. THE GOOD AND LIMITATIONS OF GOVERNMENT

Happy Government Day

April 21, 2014

On a beautiful spring Saturday I looked out my picture window at my happy neighbors, a young couple in their 30s. Bela is Hungarian and Susan is English, but here they are in America, homeowners on Long Island. Bela's parents were there with them, as they often are. It's a blessing that they live in the same town and can stop by frequently, especially since the birth of little Stanley a few months ago, Susan's first.

Another couple arrived for a visit, obviously friends. They seemed similar in age and situation. They have twins Stanley's age, and all four parents, together with Grandma and Grandpa, stood in the spring sunshine making much of the babies.

A gray-haired man pulled up in a small sport utility vehicle and got out. He lifted a tray of yellow bedding flowers from the back hatch and approached the gathering with a bright smile. They greeted each other with kisses—he's perhaps an uncle—and Susan placed the flowers carefully on the porch for planting later. And off they went together for a walk in the neighborhood.

This happy scene could unfold the way it did only because government was doing its job, providing an umbrella of protection so people could flourish together in their families and communities. For this reason, Paul told Timothy to pray for political leaders, "that we may lead a peaceful and quiet life, godly and dignified in every way" (1 Timothy 2:2).

I saw three blessings in this scene.

The first blessing was the most fundamental but also the most invisible: security. There was no sense of danger in the neighborhood, whether from other neighbors, invading armies, or even from the government itself. They could all wander off with their strollers in peace.

The second and most obvious good was family—three generations of it. With peace and security, people can live to see their grandchildren. They can enjoy the sweetest things in life, namely, folks we love and who love us in turn. Government has an important role in supporting families, protecting them from destructive burdens and not imposing unnecessary burdens, and keeping the Sabbath free and quiet. This way, moms and dads like Susan and Bela can stay together and grow old together, chiefly so that little ones like Stanley can mature into godly, pleasant, and productive adults.

Third, I saw prosperity. The chief pleasure they were enjoying was in each other, but they did so in the richness of God's creation. Stable homeownership. Reliable cars and sturdy strollers. Flowers for sharing. Government oversight of the economy without meddling interference secures people to cultivate the earth for everyone's benefit. I know that these people work hard.

God gives us richly all things ·to enjoy (1 Timothy 6:17). But to that end he also gives us government without which—confined to its proper place—there cannot be much enjoyment of anything. We have Mother's Day and Father's Day, Independence Day and Thanksgiving Day. We should also have Government Day to remind us that our civic leaders are God's servants for our good (Romans 13:3-4). Perhaps it would prompt those servants to remember their servanthood, and all of us to reflect on how under God they are called to serve.

The Happiness Platform

April 20, 2015

With the presidential nominating season under way, ideas and promises for improving our lives are filling our ears, but they tend to focus on economic issues. For example, Marco Rubio highlights tax reform, a seemingly narrow concern, while Hillary Clinton offers herself as champion of the middle class, fighting for economic opportunity against the plutocratic class that is funding her and of which she is a part.

But if you ask voters what is most important to them, their answer is always the same. Author and scholar Charles Murray has identified[1] four areas where people find deep satisfaction: family, community, vocation, and faith. People can endure a lot of hardship in life if they have a loving, stable, and supportive family. Beyond that, people's well-being depends in large part on a community that is safe and culturally stable where they have rich associations outside the family: friends, church, civic organizations, sports leagues. Good schools support family and community. Family, neighbors, and community associations are also major sources of the assurance that one is loved and respected. Beyond these things, meaningful work gives a satisfying sense of a life well-lived, that one's work matters, makes a better world. And a religious life ties all these things together with eternal purpose, shared loves, and divine assurances.

One might well object that it is not the government's business to provide us with happiness. But the way we are governed should at least make it easier for us to pursue that happiness, whether by what the government does or refrains from doing.

Public policy can either support or burden families. In some cases it can even destroy them. Tax policy is family friendly or not. Government can slow or help grow the economy, either of which has consequences for the availability and quality of employment. Financial strain weakens marriages. A robust economy makes it easier for people to match their talents with suitable work, for fathers to support a family and mothers to raise children, and for people to grow up and grow old in the same community.

So a government's focus on economics is not as narrow as it seems at first. But this can be done well or poorly. Economic policies can have clumsy and accidental consequences for people's happiness or intentionally assist it. Government that sees itself as being there simply to keep the peace—people's happiness being entirely their own business—is naïve. On the other hand, government that tries to provide happiness wherever it sees a tear is like a kindly but simpleminded giant that causes catastrophe by going too far in his attempts to help. But government by its very nature is suited to help people help themselves—whether individually, or as families, communities, associations, churches, and businesses.

The good candidate for office understands what happiness is—even in these simplest and most uncontroversial terms—and government's limited but valuable role in it. He or she will offer policies narrowly tailored to help us pursue that happiness and, beyond that, get out of the way.

Safe but Sandy-sized Government

November 5, 2012

The scale of destruction and human devastation that Superstorm Sandy brought against the northeastern United States has left many citizens grateful for governments that are big enough to handle public threats of this magnitude. Defenders of "big government" feel vindicated. But their satisfaction is unjustified on this point.

The debate between conservatives and liberals, especially in the Obama years, is often reduced to a dichotomy between big and small government, leading those on the left to think that their conservative opponents want no government at all. Anti-tax activist Grover Norquist fed that fear when he said his goal was to make government so small you could drown it in a bathtub, an ambition that's both un-Christian and unconstitutional.

The right size of government must be understood in the context of government's limited purpose and scope. God gives us government for our good (Romans 13:4), but not every good. For some goods he gives family, friendships, church, and personal responsibility, including joining with others in private organizations to accomplish larger good works.

But the things government is called to do—e.g. defense, the interstate highway system, and natural disasters so large as to be national disasters—are awesome responsibilities of grave public consequence. To deliver on these public goods, government must have power sufficient to do the task. In other words, big tasks require big power.

Alexander Hamilton in *The Federalist Papers* No. 70 wrote, "A government ill executed, whatever it may be in theory, must be, in practice, a bad government." Hamilton called this capacity for the work of government "energy." He wrote, "Energy in the executive is a leading character (sic.) in the definition of good government. It is essential to the protection of the community against foreign attacks." He also mentioned the steady administration of the laws, and the protection of property and liberty.

But in addition to energy sufficient for the legitimate and vital tasks of government, Hamilton stressed the importance of "safety." The power to secure the people is also the power to enslave them. The power to protect liberty is also the power to steal it. Our Founders deeply appreciated this problem, and the Constitution they designed, with a federal government having only limited, enumerated powers but fully empowered to execute them for the public good, is their remedy for it. When liberals talk about big government they mean just the opposite: government empowered to do anything it thinks is good … no limits apart from the Bill of Rights. But our constitution provides many more firewalls against tyranny.

That sort of "big government" government would overwhelm the Bill of Rights. It would surely be big enough to respond effectively to any hurricane. But it would be a national disaster all of its own that would devastate our liberties and with them our human dignity. Superstorm Sandy has shown us the need for big power in government. But all power must be safe power for those it is designed to help. Otherwise it's the friend that makes enemies unnecessary.

All Too Human Government

October 6, 2014

The government—especially the federal government—is comforting and scary at the same time. You like the protection it gives you, but you don't want to get on the wrong side of it.

Government seems omniscient, and that's scary too. I send in my tax return and a few weeks later they tell me I was off by $1.59. When I was a graduate student in Boston on an international visa, I was careful to stay "in status." Otherwise I was sure the INS would come knocking at my door and punt me back across the northern border. But on 9/11, I discovered, along with everyone else, that the government really doesn't know very much about who was where doing what.

Barack Obama came to power in 2009 determined to reverse that powerful dimension of the American character that views government with suspicion. But his efforts have shown us more clearly the limits of what we can expect to accomplish with that divinely established but human—all too human—instrument.

We think of the federal government as a massive, sprawling, unified entity, something like a god or an intergalactic mothership filling the sky. In fact, it's a network of people, connected institutionally and administratively, with seemingly innumerable tasks, sometimes at odds with each other. Some of those people are quite gifted, but most are just like you and me. In some ways that's reassuring. At times, it's frightening.

Our government undertakes, with the kindest motives no doubt, to reorganize our private affairs and insert its services where we should be taking responsibility ourselves.

The destructive blundering that ensues would be comical on a sitcom like *Gilligan's Island*, but it is tragic when big government causes mayhem in real lives. Consider the reach of the Obamacare system into most people's personal affairs and the utter incompetence of its rollout and execution.

The colossal blundering of the Secret Service in protecting the president is a compromise of an area that is properly the task of government. In 2011, it took a maid to discover bullet holes in a White House window four days after shots were fired. Agents heard shots at the time, but supervisors assumed it was a backfiring vehicle. Agents allowed an armed security guard with a criminal past to get into an elevator with the president in Atlanta. A crazed man hopped the White House fence, crossed the lawn, entered the front door of the executive mansion, and ran around inside before he was finally tackled. No dogs. No sniper. And the alarm system had been muted because it had been sounding off a lot and bothering the White House staff.

To the human fallibility you can add the human tendency to self-serving abuse of power. Running a hospital system for our veterans seems straightforward. But people died and others languished in pain so administrators could claim they met their legally mandated turnover rates. Public servants pursue their interests and cover their tails.

Yes, these people are all too much like you and me. It seems reasonable to conclude, therefore, that the more of each of our lives that can be left to our own fallible discretion and the less that is entrusted to people in government of ordinary competence and all too ordinary self-regard, the better it will be for all of us.

2. THE DIVIDE IN GOVERNMENT

Our Domestic Cold War

March 4, 2013

America is more ideologically divided than ever. The country as a whole is deeply divided on everything from the nature of wealth creation and the purpose of government even to what marriage is. Red states and blues states, the cultural elite and the street, the city and the sticks: it seems that we inhabit different moral universes and we don't even share a common language. Michael Barone[2] describes America as two countries that are not even on speaking terms. To echo Alisdair MacIntyre, our politics has become civil war carried on by other means.[3]

America as a country, as a national political community, cannot continue if this divide continues to deepen. Harmony is essential to community. Strife destroys it. As things stand, we can't move forward in economic growth, border security, world leadership, or anything until we come to greater agreement as neighbors and fellow citizens.

But that harmonious unity is elusive. A political community wants to be one and at rest within itself, a kind of universal friendship. Everyone helps. Everyone trusts and is trustworthy. But social harmony, unlike our present rancor, is also more than that. In *The Republic*, Socrates concludes that "that city [is] best governed that is most like a single human being," literally a body politic. It wants to function organically the way a body moves in flowing coordination under the brain's government, every part taking pleasure in fulfilling its part. But where do you see that?

And yet this is precisely the way Romans 12 describes life in the church, the body of Christ, the Kingdom of God which is God's new society. "For just as the body is one and has many members, and all the members of the body, though many, are one body, so it is with Christ." When Christ has finished his redeeming work in the new creation, our life together will be that perfect harmonious unity. "If one member suffers, all suffer together; if one member is honored, all rejoice together" (I Cor. 12:12, 26).

Of course, that is a marvelous, eschatological reality, God's sovereign, recreative work at the end of sinful history. But in the meantime, there are ordinary, human means for living in greater peace: strong families, sensible education, free markets, the rule of law, and wise statesmanship at the top. But God also anticipates his final work in his present grace. The love and Spirit of Christ brings His church into to ever greater harmony and unity. As "the salt of the earth" and "the light of the world" (Matt. 5:13-16), Christians can bring our communities into greater concord by our Christian example and influence. Thus, "Blessed are the peacemakers" (Matt. 5:9).

A Choice Between Two Americas

November 4, 2013

The Affordable Care Act passed with no Republican votes. Since then, popular opposition to it has polled consistently above 50 percent. From its inception, Obamacare has exposed the fault lines within American politics. Supporters and opponents of the law have fundamentally different views of what politics is, of what government and civic community are.

The views expressed in our Declaration of Independence and embodied in our Constitution advocate limited government. From the start, America has been a brilliantly ambitious political experiment. It attempts to solve the great problem of government, which is, as James Madison put it in *The Federalist Papers* No. 51, how to enable the government to restrain the governed and at the same time oblige it to restrain itself. We need government to protect us from each other and from foreign invaders, but the power to protect is also the power to enslave. Fundamental to this Founding American spirit is a historically justified distrust of government, and thus an extremely guarded embrace of it.

Government is like a gun. Many see the need to have one in their house for protection, but they keep it in a gun safe, albeit handy, with a safety lock on it. Only the most trusted and capable people in the home are allowed to handle it.

But while gun safety is the norm among gun users, people today who share this cautious approach to the use of government are called "conservatives," and in Washington, D.C., they are vilified as radicals. Why? Because for more than a century our politics have been divided by a "substitute Founding" led by people like Woodrow Wilson, Franklin Roosevelt, and now Barack Obama. Our nation is so politically divided because—within the same country, under the same Constitution—there are two different Americas struggling to establish themselves: One is "republican" and the other is "progressive."

In 1944, President Roosevelt announced the inadequacy of the existing Constitution to protect liberty in the industrial age, saying it requires the redistributionist welfare state.[4] Columnist George Will points out that "the name 'progressivism' implies criticism of the Founding, which we leave behind as we make progress."[5]

Progressives trust government implicitly, hence their reflexive willingness to empower it. They believe in governing human affairs not by private judgment, local communities, and prudent statesmen, but by applying the discoveries of social science by administrative elites, or technocrats, in the interest of general peace, safety, and comfort. This leaves only a grudging allowance for personal liberty and self-government. It is the Environmental Protection Agency writ large. Hence, though you were told, "If you like your health insurance plan you can keep it," Obamacare sees no problem with telling you what plan you are allowed to like.

This explains why, when the Tea Party wants to roll back the personal security state, progressives like Nancy Pelosi hear a call to destroy government itself. Tomorrow is Election Day. Our choice in every election is between which America we want to be.

The Political Big Rock Candy Mountain

June 22, 2012   *Weah*

The problem with liberals is they don't like the way the world is. Now, there is a sense in which we all share that dissatisfaction. Sin has made a wreck of the world and of each of our lives, and it's a mark of good character to recognize that and rebel against it. But liberals and conservatives differ in their attitudes toward the nature of things as God created them to be. There is an order of creation that is good and that no one can violate without unhappy consequences. It is the way things work, not only physically, but also morally.

Against nature, political liberals advocate same-sex marriage and they want women fighting fires, fighting in wars, and doing all the manliest things alongside the hardest men. They believe that overcoming natural sexual distinctions is progress, i.e., that it's not only possible and permissible, but also desirable. But as the old saying goes, "God always forgives (when asked through Christ), people sometimes forgive, nature never forgives."

This divinely established order also governs the effective creation and just distribution of wealth. But liberals want broadly distributed prosperity simply by government imposition. Anyone who questions this system of well-intentioned giveaways they call "heartless," even though in the end it produces the very suffering it was intended to relieve.

Ten years ago, Congress forced private banks to give mortgages to people who could not afford houses. Nature took its course, gave us a housing bubble, and then the system imploded. Sadly, where I live, the concentrations of foreclosed homes are all in poorer, minority neighborhoods. With friends like these in Congress, who needs enemies?

In your personal life, you know that you have to live within limits. Though you need a host of good things—a nice vacation after a trying year, bodywork on your rusting but still running car, siding for your aging home, generous gifts for neighbors and relatives in need—if you just spend your way down the list, you go broke. You could borrow the money, but there are limits to what you can finance. People who spend on impulse, whether noble or selfish, without regard for these limits go bankrupt.

All too often, a liberal in Congress is someone who doesn't recognize any natural limitations to government spending on entitlements and social programs. If there is a human need, there must be a corresponding government program, and the national line of credit is endless. Never mind that the need is naturally addressed by family, neighbor, or church. In its attempt to defy the laws of economic gravity, this "progressive" approach to economic justice must eventually end in national bankruptcy as we have seen in Europe, a moderate example, and communism, an extreme one.

There is a limit to how long you can pretend the world is a big rock candy mountain "where the handouts grow on bushes."

> In the Big Rock Candy Mountains,
> There's a land that's fair and bright,
> Where the handouts grow on bushes
> And you sleep out every night.
> Where the boxcars all are empty
> And the sun shines every day
> And the birds and the bees
> And the cigarette trees
> The lemonade springs
> Where the bluebird sings
> In the Big Rock Candy Mountains.
>
> …In the Big Rock Candy Mountains,
> The jails are made of tin.
> And you can walk right out again,
> As soon as you are in.
> There ain't no short-handled shovels,
> No axes, saws nor picks,
> I'm bound to stay
> Where you sleep all day,
> Where they hung the jerk
> That invented work
> In the Big Rock Candy Mountains.[6]

The American People's Gridlock

July 14, 2014

Everyone's down on Congress. Public approval for the institution stands around 13 percent. Even three billionaires—Sheldon Adelson, Warren Buffet, and Bill Gates—whom the law generally serves well, used an op-ed page[7] to voice their frustration with Capitol Hill's extraordinary inability to pass needed legislation.

Congress is certainly no remake of *Let's Make a Deal*. People call them childish, a deliberative daycare center. But most of them are highly accomplished and very shrewd when it comes to preserving their jobs.

Congress is divided because the country is divided. Vermont is not New Hampshire; Wyoming is not Oregon. Pennsylvania is deeply divided between the big cities—Philly and Pittsburgh—and everything in between. And these places do not just lean a little one way and the other; they have radically different ways of seeing the world, the people who inhabit it, and our hope for the future.

Consider abortion. Some see it as the legalized slaughter of our children, a national abomination that in time is sure to bring God's wrath. Others see it as a noble right, essential to women's equal liberty and worth defending at any cost. A sad and angry woman in Columbus, Ohio, caught on video confronting pro-life demonstrators,[8] dramatizes the conflict. She tries to be as violent as she can with words alone to punish these people for entering the debate. Then she gets physically violent. Abortion divides Democrats and Republicans almost neatly along party lines.

Consider the anger generated over the *Burwell v. Hobby Lobby* Supreme Court decision. In the midst of a national controversy over the minimum wage, Hobby Lobby voluntarily pays its full-time employees $13 an hour! But because this company refuses to pay for employees' access through insurance to four forms of abortion-inducing birth control, it may as well be the cruelest faction of the Taliban throwing acid in women's faces.

Consider homosexuality. Those who advocate its normalization, even to the point of legally recognizing same-sex relationships as marriage, ferociously attack anyone who questions their behavior morally as though they just stepped through a time warp from the 13th century. Those who dissent from the post-Christian cultural experiment, including polygamy and transgenderism, see the utter confusion of its giddy embrace destroying the family and every good that depends on it. Polarized views in Congress reflect this sort of cultural polarization among the states and districts represented.

A meme of side-by-side photos depicting a young woman standing in front of the Stars and Stripes holding a gun and a Bible and a Palestinian female terrorist holding a gun and a Quran illustrates the broad divide. The caption reads, "Explain the Difference." Many Americans can't see the difference between someone standing in front of freedom's flag holding the benefits of the First and Second Amendments and a jihadist who blew herself up, killing four innocent people. Our borders contain two completely different moral universes.

This Congress is our Congress. We elected these men and women. The problem is us before it is them. But I'm not giving up on Jesus, the Constitution, and the least among us. I don't see moral passion subsiding on the hard left. Only a surprising work of God can make us one country again.

Pride and Shame on Independence Day

July 7, 2014

Independence Day is a flag-waving, love-of-country time to reflect on everything good about America. So the recent Pew poll that asked people if they often feel proud to be American is well-timed. Fifty-six percent of us often do.[9] But thoughtful patriots pause before answering this question. What is it to be American? What is America? Can you be down on America but still proud to be American? Can you love your country if your country loves what it should not love?

I became a citizen in 2010[10] after studying and working in this country for 25 years as a Canadian. I am proud to be American, but not always proud of America. Consider the people who are dearest to us. We love them without fail, but we are not always proud of them, depending on how they use or neglect their talents.

The United States is a country founded on just principles: "We hold these truths to be self-evident, that all men are created equal; that they are endowed by their Creator with certain unalienable rights; that among these are Life, Liberty, and the pursuit of Happiness." The nation is continually rising up to "live out the true meaning of its creed," or on some points stumbling and falling backward. We cannot be proud of our stumblings.

America is a land of enormous creative energy: culturally, economically, and technologically. At home, we are generally decent and compassionate. We're combative, but within limits. We are still a church-going, gospel-preaching, missionary-sending land of religious liberty—though we often mix the gospel with error, commercialism, and self-focus. Abroad, we feed the world's people, aid them in disaster, and do what we can to relieve their all-too-often miserable estate. Even by simply pursuing our interests, we are a beacon of freedom, a constraint on tyrants.

But in America, it is a constitutional right to kill your baby in what should be the safety of the womb. Large and powerful segments of the population are passionately committed to this court-invented political right. Since 1973, we have murdered almost 57 million of our own people in this way. The Pew poll found that "about half of the public (51%) says abortion should be legal in all or most cases." It is also telling that the especially barbaric practice of partial-birth abortion is even a subject of debate.

Add to this a national and culturally dominant war on manhood, womanhood, family, and marriage and it's hard to glow about this "land that I love" without significant qualification.

America lives always in a state of aspiration, facing the gap between our practice and our principles. We are never fully what we want to be, not always mindful of what we should be, and sometimes shamefully in denial of what God, nature, and our forefathers have taught us.

Can we be proud while the gap exists? But it will always exist—at times larger, at times smaller. "Grateful" is actually a better word than proud. Pride is unjustly satisfied. Gratitude is humble and hungry to be always more worthy of the patriot's love. It directs us to God, lifts us out of self and the narrow horizon of the present, and leaves us mindful of our shortcomings. Perhaps an annual Repentance Day—a day of silence and fasting—would help us.

3. THE VOTERS

Voters are Still Looking for Hope
October 12, 2015

There's no incumbent in the 2016 race for the White House, so it's a jump ball in both political parties. The surprises on both sides have been the clamor for outsiders. In the GOP, half the primary voters prefer Ben Carson, Carly Fiorina, or, first among them, Donald Trump, none of whom has ever held elective office. On the Democratic side, Bernie Sanders, who's an Independent in the U.S. Senate, poses a daunting challenge to the virtually anointed Hillary Clinton.

Though Trump and Sanders, a real estate magnate and a Vermont socialist, seem polar opposites, they both respond to a growing concern that political and economic life in America has become stiflingly unfair: We're losing the American dream, the rich and privileged control the system to their own advantage leaving ordinary people helpless, and politicians ask for voter support then serve big donors who in turn own them.

Trump says he understands this complaint because he was one of those owners. He argues that because he himself is rich—quite very rich, actually—he can't be bought and will therefore serve ordinary people as political leaders should. Internationally, Trump claims we're being suckered with bad trade deals by foreign governments because our leaders either cannot or do not look out for us. They're serving themselves and their friends with "free trade."

Sanders appeals to a parallel sentiment on the political left. These people also have the sense that America is not a fair game anymore: The system is rigged in favor of the 1 percent, the few wealthiest. Sanders' website laments "the growing gap between the very rich and everyone else," and, "the enormous economic and political power of the billionaire class," and the "economic and political oligarchy" that we kid ourselves is our democracy.

But whereas the disaffected on the right believe that big government in collusion with corporate elites has killed the dream, the left looks to government to revive it. So Sanders would use Washington to force the pieces back into place: guaranteed paid sick leave, universal healthcare, free higher education, and big spending federal job creation. A government-driven Nerf economy would guarantee that no one suffers and no one falls behind.

But would anyone care about income inequality if they had the sense that they and others could rise with honest hard work? People want a return of the America where the circumstances of your birth don't determine your destiny, a country where people can rise from rags to riches, or at least to modest middle-class comfort with a car, a backyard, and a college education for your kids who will live better than you did.

Supporters of both of these political populists are looking for hope, what Barack Obama promised and did not deliver. Instead, we got record profits for Wall Street and a sluggish recovery for the rest of us too many of whom cling by our fingertips to the bottom edge of the middle class. In America, we find hope in opportunity, and we expect opportunity in a free system. It is an open question whether either of these candidates, or any of the others, has the key to making real the promises of our great experiment in self-government and human dignity.

Why Do We Keep Buying What Politicians are Selling?
July 29, 2013

Sales is an honorable profession. A good salesman connects people who have needs with good products and services that can help them. Both sides benefit. But in a fallen world where people treat each other as means instead of ends, and seek to profit themselves at other peoples' expense instead of serving their needs, we view people who are "selling something" with justified suspicion. Car salesmen come to mind, especially used car salesmen, not a few of whom are keen to sell you more than you need, more than you can afford, and less than you think you are getting.

People view politicians as "selling something," but not as often as they should. Every four years they come into office promising the most honest, most open administration in history, unlike the previous crowd, but they always end up behaving like the previous crowd. It is well that Congress has only a 12 percent public-approval rating, but disappointing that there are so many "safe" seats one election to the next.

It is because so many politicians behave like unscrupulous salesmen that long election campaigns and aggressive media scrutiny are so important to the public good. Sometimes politicians are selling an amazing cure-all, and sometimes they're only selling themselves. As voters listening to political assurances, we are often as helpless as an average car owner confronted by a mechanic with our dangerously worn, reverberated thingamajig: $2,000 or you will surely die. The internet has helped us in navigating the mysteries of both spheres.

The leaders of the city of Detroit, both civic and union, told their constituents they would slay the big shots for them and deliver generous benefits free of charge at someone else's expense for a long retirement after years of high wages. Now the city is bankrupt, but the seats at every level likely are still considered politically safe for the party in power. In 2008, Barack Obama sold himself with a sunny slogan, then in office sold us health insurance reform promising 30 percent more at 25 percent off, or some blowout special like that.

As much as we like a solid district or state, colored according to our political preferences, a seriously contested election is good not only for the public interest but also for keeping our favorite politicians honest. This is also why a press corps that has become as critical of the political leadership as a tween at a Justin Bieber concert or a cardinal at a papal audience is dangerous to the hopes of any political enthusiast.

The Spirited Citizen

April 20, 2012

Metaphor Political anger is high these days. From Trump and Sanders rallies to Black Lives Matter demonstrations, it's like we have a collective bee in the mouth.[1] But we should not let it discourage us. As Finley Peter Dunne put it, "Politics ain't beanbag."

In politics, the stakes are high. While there is a common good we all share, there is also my good, or what I think is my good, that needs defending against my neighbors. People steal from each other not only with guns and crowbars and with shady business practices, but also with political power. They can take your property as well as what you treasure about our life together. Maybe it's a development project that's robbing you, or same-sex marriage. That's when what Merle

Haggard calls "the fightin' side of me" comes out, and angry citizens get political. Harvey Mansfield, in his brilliant essay about politics and political passions, wrote, "Politics is about what makes you angry. ... People go into politics to pick a fight, not to avoid one."[12]

The Greeks had a name for this political anger, thumos! It is the most characteristically political passion, the spirited defense of one's own, but intimately connected with a claim to what one believes is right. It joins what is most particular ("me") with what is most universal ("right"). It's what gives engagement to the citizen, courage to the soldier, and ambition to the statesman. It's what fires up the patriot to cling to his liberties, and bark warnings about his cold, dead hands. The spirit of liberty and thus the defense of one's dignity is that thumotic spirit that bristles under the banner, "Don't tread on me." C. S. Lewis, in *The Abolition of Man*, wrote that thumos, the seat of moral seriousness, is what makes us human.

So, in the months leading up to the election, if you find yourself shocked that political debate is not like a living room conversation or an academic discussion, remember that these political combatants are taking themselves and justice seriously, even if they're not always right. That's politics.

4. THE CANDIDATES

Political Good Shepherds

August 24, 2012

As the November elections approach and difficult choices confront us, we would do well to think about Jesus, the King of kings and perfect ruler of the nations. He is not an unreasonable standard for judging candidates for American political office because He is the standard to which God, who establishes and judges all the rulers of the earth, will hold them.

It is an ancient tradition to view rulers as shepherds of their people. In John 10, Christ calls Himself a Good Shepherd and shows what that means for good government.

We see first that a good political leader is not one who seeks to be served, but one whose chief desire is to serve. "The good shepherd lays down his life for the sheep" (John 10:11). When we hold some sort of power over our neighbors (as parent, manager, or senator), even the best of us find it tempting to serve ourselves even at the expense of those we govern, to serve our selfish interests rather than the common good. But that's the definition of tyrannical government, and the opposite of the way Jesus governs.

Second, by the Good Shepherd standard, a good political leader is one who knows his people. The Good Shepherd knows His sheep and they know Him in turn (John 10:14). Jesus means more than academic knowledge because He cites the example of the mutual knowledge within the Godhead. It's a personal knowledge that comes from experience with one another and includes mutual affection. Government is not an abstract application of principles. To govern wisely, a ruler must know his people and have sympathy and affection for their way of life. The prospect of someone from Brooklyn governing Iowans for their good is not promising, and vice versa. Good government requires something like the bonds of friendship as opposed to a stance of enmity, distrust, or contempt. Niccolo Machiavelli, a man whose name has been virtually synonymous with the devil for almost 400 years, advised that a prince should have no other thought but thoughts of war … even in domestic government! If an officeholder sees the people simply as obstacles to his or her reelection and rising, the people should select another candidate.

Lastly, the example of Christ the Good Shepherd teaches us that a good political leader does not divide or scatter his people, but unifies them. Good shepherding gathers "one flock" out of diverse sheep (John 10:16). Christ unified Jews and Gentiles in His church, people between whom there was strong cultural hostility. An ambitious churchman in the young church, if he were a bad shepherd, could have exploited this factional divide for political advantage. Our political leaders can do this by exploiting differences in wealth, race, age, or sex. It's a sign of using political authority to serve oneself, not the people. Presidents often come to office saying they want to be the president of all Americans, not just of those who voted for them. But the selfish politics of division soon takes over.

We will never have perfectly Christlike leadership this side of the Lord's return. But through our votes, Christian citizens can encourage it to the extent we make Christ our measure when sizing up the candidates for office.

Characteristics of a Candidate

August 3, 2015

Republican primary voters in 2015 have lots of choices in this presidential election cycle—17 so far: nine governors, five senators, two business executives, and a surgeon. On the Democratic side, there are only five announced candidates: two governors, two senators, and one senator/secretary of state. It is tempting to favor the person who best voices one's own disgruntlements or who has the best policy positions. But good government is more than charm or ideological purity.

Electing a president is an awesome responsibility. God raises up rulers and He brings them down (Daniel 2:21), but He uses natural and human means. In a republic, He uses the consent of the people expressed constitutionally through elections. In this case, it is not only the rulers who need political wisdom but voters too. In his philosophical classic, *The Politics* (Book V, chapter 9), Aristotle helps us with four characteristics of a good political leader.

The first is "affection for the regime." Call it patriotism. A ruler must love the country he or she aspires to lead and its system of government. President Obama began his presidency apologizing for the country and has never stopped. So we must ask: Does the candidate have a record of serving community and country or of self-promotion?

The second is "capacity for the work." An effective president must bring people together, build coalitions, and achieve compromise that doesn't allow the perfect to be enemy of the good. This takes governing experience. To pass laws, senators have to work with each other, even across party lines. Governors have to manage an administration as well as legislators in their own party and in the opposition's, and they are responsible for the results.

That capacity includes the gift of rhetoric or persuasion: well-chosen, well-spoken words that move people to agreement and action. A president's best ideas are useless if he can't make them understandable and compelling for the public and rally a majority to the best course of action.

The work also requires prudence—having not only true principles but also the ability to apply them wisely within the practical constraints of a fallen world. Prudence requires experience. Youthful candidates and sideline opinionators don't have it.

The third characteristic is "virtue." Contrary to what Gov. Bill Clinton's supporters told us in 1992, the president's job is inseparable from his moral character. Important traits include humility, trustworthiness, and self-control. Does the candidate have a strong marriage and family? How does he handle the truth? Is he cavalier about the legality of killing babies in abortion? Is he at all concerned about the poor and the weak? Does he fear God? In general, is there a record of principled disposition toward what is right?

The fourth is "justice." Aristotle means a willingness to abide by the rule of law. The current president has demonstrated impatience with constitutional restraints on his power, used executive orders in place of legislation, and selectively ignored laws. As a habit, does the candidate do what he wants to do or what he ought to do?

God gives us government for our good, but securing the common good for a people is no easy task. Does your favorite in the field have the talent, character, and preparation it takes?

The Greatness America Needs

March 21, 2016

Donald Trump says we need to make America great again. He talks about diplomatic and commercial deal-making abroad and tightening illegal immigration at home. But it is generations of assaults on our families, our churches, and our schools that have crippled America's capacity for greatness. These are the three pillars that support a people in great civilizational accomplishment.

American greatness grows out of healthy American families. Strong fathers, devoted mothers, and resilient marriages cultivate successive generations of creative, constructive Americans. In love, these parents deliver the tens of thousands of lessons, restrictions, rebukes, and examples that steer their children out of the foolishness of youth into stable, productive maturity; out of the self-indulgence of childhood into the self-discipline of adulthood. Family is the incubator of character and seedbed of civilization.

Full and faithful churches make America great. A faithful church is where we learn humility, to serve God first, neighbor second, and oneself last. It helps cultivate in each of us an "internal policeman," good character that is essential to a free and stable society. The more that people are internally disposed to mutual respect and mutual help (Ezekiel 36:27), the less need there is for government power that can be abused, whether in blue police uniforms or gray administrative buildings. There can be no greatness except for a free people, and no political freedom where the flesh widely has sway.

Public schools would advance American greatness if they would effectively teach not only reading, writing, math, and science (which, despite spending more than $600 billion annually, they do not), but also teach the greatness of the American system of political, economic, and religious liberty. The passionate enthusiasm of many young people for the coddling government gospel of a Vermont socialist can be explained largely by the failure of American schools to explain the genius, dignity, and aspirations of the American experiment in popular self-government.

When people faithfully attend Sunday worship (I cannot speak to what happens in synagogues, mosques, and temples), there is an overflow to families. When children are schooled in the Bible, they are better students in school.

The current candidates are not addressing these issues,

though Marco Rubio spoke about the priority of the family and Ted Cruz has revived the Reagan-era idea of abolishing the U.S. Department of Education. There isn't much government can do to make healthy churches, but it can protect their freedom to be churches and it can respect their vital role in a flourishing life. The Democratic candidates seem at best indifferent to the further crumbling of all three pillars.

The call to greatness is a call to a kind of resurrection. What once stood tall and full of vigor is laid low and lifeless, seemingly lost to the past. We are asking if these national bones can live again (Ezekiel 37:3). Our political resurrection requires policy changes in these areas at every level, but will not be complete or lasting without the power that flows from Resurrection Sunday.

—Section II—
THE ISSUES

1. SECURITY

The Blessing of Terror-free Routine

December 7, 2015

Looking out the window of the morning commuter train as we pulled toward Jamaica Station in Queens, N.Y., I watched, as I often do, the streets slowly coming alive with human movement. Tired people walking to their jobs, running errands, or keeping an appointment. In the shadow of Thanksgiving and of the monstrous and altogether surprising massacre in San Bernardino, the simple scene was heavy with significance. The fact that nothing unusual was happening moved me to quiet rejoicing. No chaos. No blood in the streets. Several years after 9/11, I would still look with tense anticipation at any plane flying overhead and would thank God every time I arrived safely at Penn Station.

And here we are again. But now the terror—the general anticipation of unexpected and random violent evil—has broadened. GOP presidential candidate and New Jersey Gov. Chris Christie told the Republican Jewish Coalition, "If a center for the developmentally disabled in San Bernardino, Calif., can be a target for a terrorist attack, then every place in America is a target for a terrorist attack."

He didn't mention the other side of that new breadth of possibility, but many have it in mind even if they don't speak it. If this apparently ordinary, American-born, Muslim environmental health specialist, recently married with a 6-month-old baby, can gun down dozens of his co-workers at a staff meeting, then people are bound to be wary of just about anyone who is or appears to be Muslim. Because of Syed Farook and Tashfeen Malik, almost all Muslims in this country will suffer the injustice of this apprehension.

President Obama had this in mind as he delivered his Oval Office speech following the San Bernardino attack. But in calling us to reject that fear conscientiously, he did not address Farook's apparent ordinariness or the liberal bad conscience that made Farook's neighbors unwilling to report suspicious activity around his house. It's complicated.

The Apostle Paul told us to pray for all those in authority to the end that we may lead peaceful and quiet lives in all dignity and godliness (1 Timothy 2:2). Much of life is a dull blessing, a blessing in its dullness. A short drive through familiar streets. A long red light. Buying coffee. Taking out the trash. A quiet evening watching home renovation TV shows. At the Inland Regional Center in San Bernardino, a gathering of unremarkable people expected another dull, semiannual meeting with speeches and pastries.

The New York Daily News raised a howl of objection to political leaders offering prayer in place of stricter gun control laws. "God Isn't Fixing This," read the headlines that filled the front page. "As latest batch of innocent Americans are left lying in pools of blood, cowards who could truly end gun scourge continue to hide behind meaningless platitudes." They had in mind leaders such as Speaker of the House Paul Ryan, who tweeted: "We all are thinking about what happened in California today. Please keep the victims & their families in your prayers."

The connection between gun control and lowering criminal gun violence is controversial. But when you scorn prayer for peace to the God of peace, you scorn much. So we pray once more for the ordinary to be uneventful. And we thank God, as we should, when our ordinary days end with sleepy regularity.

The Refugee Crisis of Faith

September 7, 2015

What would we do if hundreds of thousands of people from an alien land were streaming across our borders seeking asylum from the ravages of war and merciless oppression? This is what Europe is facing from Syria, Afghanistan, and Eritrea. Germany expects 800,000 asylum-seekers 2015 alone, a fourfold increase over the previous year.

And you can't blame them for trying. The Apostle Paul told Timothy to pray for rulers so that we may live peaceful, quiet lives in all godliness and dignity (I Timothy 2:1-2).

But most of Syria is a choice between the tyrant Bashar al-Assad, who gases his own people, and the ISIS monsters. So it's no surprise that so many are braving every peril of the unknown to reach stable, prosperous Europe. They love their children and their lives.

But many fear that Islam is accomplishing demographically[13] what it failed for a thousand years to do militarily: Conquer Christian Europe or, one might say, a now largely secular Europe of empty churches and pagan laws. In Western Europe, the Muslim population is highest in France at 7.5 percent, but these populations are concentrated in cities where they have greater social visibility and disproportionate political influence. In addition, their birthrates are dramatically higher. This fear expresses itself partly by support for right-wing, reactionary political parties like the National Front in France.

But Christians do not fear. Though events may surprise us, the Lord views them with calm because He sovereignly oversees them. It was He who turned the armies of the Turks back from the gates of 17th century Vienna but gave Constantinople, now Istanbul, into their hands. God who tells the waves of the sea, "Thus far shall you come, and no farther, and here shall your proud waves be stayed" (Job 38:11), also directs the movements of peoples and the affections of their hearts.

I was surprised last week (to my shame) to read about remarkable conversions to Christ among the Muslim Syrian refugees in Germany. The Lord who brought the Ethiopian eunuch to Philip in the desert (Acts 8:26-40) can bring Middle Eastern Muslims to Himself in spiritually blighted Europe. Is there mercy yet for the rebellious continent of Christendom's glory? It would be just like the God of hopeless cases to turn the wayward descendants of the Reformation back to Himself through a deluge of Muslims who had been scourged by pious allies of the Islamic Republic of Iran and mauled by the Koranic purists of the Islamic State.

European Union President and former Polish Prime Minister Donald Tusk said in reference to this crisis, "Referring to Christianity in a public debate on migration must mean in the first place the readiness to show solidarity and sacrifice. For a Christian it shouldn't matter what race, religion and nationality the person in need represents." That is to say, Christians are confident by faith that if we seek first the Kingdom of God in love, God will faithfully provide for us (Matthew 6:33).

If all you have is a culture, then large numbers of people from other cultures endanger what you are. But if what you have is Christ, then if you welcome the refugee in faithful obedience to God's law of love, a Christian people can be confident that God will honor that service and bless them in surprising ways.

The Refugee Crisis Conundrum

November 30, 2015

The refugee crisis in Europe and the proper American response to it is a conundrum. And anyone who suggests what we should do without recognizing the conundrum—the perplexing tension between the demands of charity and security—should not be taken seriously.

President Obama has proposed that we accept 10,000 refugees. Canada has pledged to take 25,000. Germany expects 800,000 this year. Balkan states are closing their borders or passing the migrants through as quickly as possible. But the Syrian civil war and the people desperately fleeing it are half a world away. Is it even our problem?

God expects his image bearers to love one another. "Love your neighbor as yourself" (Lev. 19:18). But, to be fair, neighbor obligation is qualified by circumstances. One has greater responsibility for the neighbor at hand than the one on the other side of the globe. One's capacity to help also makes a difference. If I cannot swim, I am not responsible for jumping in to save a drowning man. Jordan is morally obliged to help the Syrian refugees, but its limited means reduce its obligation. Germany has greater means—wealth, organizational infrastructure, and a Christian moral heritage—but it is farther away and has a problem integrating its current Muslim population. America has great means—material and moral—and great logistical capacity to bridge the ocean divide. Though the suffering in our midst are not the far-flung suffering, capacity entails responsibility.

Yet the cause of the refugee crisis itself complicates it with legitimate security concerns. Monstrous, resourceful people ideologically devoted to indiscriminate mass murder will surely use this pitiful exodus as a Trojan horse for infiltrating the West with jihadis. Screening the refugees is difficult as there is no data available from the Syrian government to help us. Some suggest we accept only Christians, or at least prefer them, others that we exclude young unmarried men.

There is a middle course to explore. Syria is not a prison that people have been looking for an excuse to escape. It takes the threat of death or destitution to dislodge people from their native land in these numbers. So given that it would be better for all concerned if these displaced people could stay in their own countries, or at least their own regions, the United States could, as some have suggested, establish safe zones within Syria and Iraq. We would have to enforce it as a no-fly zone and protect it with troops. Robert Kagan of the Brookings Institution suggests 30,000 ground troops initially, soon replaced by a coalition of European and Middle Eastern forces.[14] (Destroying ISIS and declawing Damascus is another matter.) We could also generously assist good neighbors like Jordan with much of what they need for their refugee camps.

To whom much is given, much is required (Luke 12:48). A nation with a rich Christian heritage should extend itself in love. But a government must first protect the people under its care. This balance of charity with security is the task for the Solomons in Washington, if there are any.

2. Foreign Policy

Why the "America First" Pitch Resonates

May 2, 2016

Donald Trump's "America first" speech, his first major foreign policy speech on April 27th, though filled with contradictions,[15] only added to his appeal with voters as he distinguishes himself from his two predecessors in the White House and his likely opponent. Regardless of the actual history, many Americans are sick of what they see as our leaders putting the country second or themselves first: President George W. Bush's "America to the rescue" policy, President Obama's policy of "American passivity," and former Secretary of State Clinton's history of "America for sale."

Voters associate Bush's neo-Wilsonian policy of creating Middle Eastern democracies with a long and expensive war that in the end seems to have bought us chaos in the region, Iranian dominance, and leaking terrorism. Obama's reckless and premature withdrawal from Iraq is more arguably the cause of those problems, but voter perception is what matters in this case. People are tired of spending American blood and treasure, as they see it, so that purple-fingered Iraqis can squander the chance at liberty for which they should have risked their own lives.

Seven years of Obama's policy of American withdrawal under the cover of a phony "leading from behind" has many voters livid, especially on the right. Indifference to a dead ambassador and empty red-line threats have constrained our ability to defend our interests by alienating our allies (Europe, Saudi Arabia), emboldening our enemies (Russia, Iran, China), and earning us the contempt of even small nations.[16]

Infamous $235,000 speeches by Bill and Hillary Clinton to corporations and at least one country with business before the U.S. government anticipate that Mrs. Clinton, if elected, may well subordinate national interests to her personal pockets and funding the Clinton Foundation at a time when Americans are feeling especially sold out by their political leaders.

So when Trump says, "America first will be the major and overriding theme of my administration," it resonates with voters.

God established government for the good of the people it governs, for their liberty, prosperity, and moral flourishing, not for the enrichment of those who rule or the benefit of other countries at the expense of one's own. Despite the shortcomings of both the candidate and his speech, Trump touches on an important truth. God's love-of-neighbor ethic also governs nations that are, after all, communities of individuals. But that same love requires nations, which are essential to people's well-being, to preserve themselves in a dangerous and competitive world.

The Putin Enigma

March 10, 2014

Even though Russian President Vladimir Putin has controlled his country for 15 years, we are still unclear on what sort of man he is. A newly inaugurated George W. Bush looked him in the eye, got a "sense of his soul," and found him "straightforward and trustworthy." When Hillary Clinton took office as secretary of state she pulled her "reset button" stunt, forgiving Russia's invasion of neighboring Georgia the previous year but with no indication that Russia would behave differently. President Obama, unaware of a live microphone under his nose, whispered to Putin's instrument, President Dmitri Medvedev, that he would have "more flexibility" to co-operate in missile defense negotiations after his reelection.

Now that Putin is sending troops westward into Eastern Europe, people are eager to figure out his character and ambitions.

Matthew Kaminski argues that Putin is moving against Kiev's Maidan revolution because Ukraine has become "the alternative to the Russian authoritarian project."[17] Putin's domestic project seems to have even wider international dimensions. In 2005, he told the Russian Parliament that the disintegration of the Soviet Union was the "greatest geopolitical disaster" of the 20th century. This together with military and economic flexing on the Russian frontier suggest a Putinist plan to reestablish the old empire. Robert Zubrin claims that Putin, a former KGB agent, is not a repositioned communist but a "Eurasianist" who is building a new form of totalitarian state that combines elements of communism, Nazism, ecologism, and traditionalism.[18]

Whatever he is, Putin is a Machiavellian, and anyone who reads him otherwise becomes his "useful idiot." The Machiavellian ruler artfully combines the lion and the fox, perfecting the use of force and fraud. Putin invaded Crimea with thousands of troops, but stripped them of identifying Russian insignia and claimed they were all "local self-defense forces." The perfect fraud requires "coloring" one's crimes so they appear justified.

Machiavelli wrote in *The Prince* (chapter 19),

> ... the one who has known best how to use the fox has come out best. But it is necessary to know well how to color this nature, and to be a great pretender and dissembler ... and he who deceives will always find someone who will let himself be deceived.

So Putin moved on the pretext of aiding the Russian-speaking minority in eastern Ukraine who were suffering "intimidation and terror." He said, "Russia cannot ignore calls for help and it acts accordingly, in full compliance with international law," though there have been no reported incidents against Russian speakers and he claims he has no troops in Crimea.

Putin presents himself as a deeply religious man who treasures the crucifix his mother gave him, a defender of international law, and opponent of extreme nationalists, neo-Nazis, and anti-Semites. Machiavelli counseled that a prince "should appear all mercy, all faith, all honesty, all humanity, all religion." Appear ... not be. Putin understands that.

On a playground, it is fairly hopeless to encourage friendliness in bullies by treating them as friends or to encourage trustworthiness by trusting them. In international politics, especially with characters like Vladimir Putin, it is calamitous.

3. IMMIGRATION

An Aggressive Immigration Agenda

December 24, 2012

Men of Mexican or Central American origin congregate at an intersection where pick-up trucks and minivans arrive early each day in search of workers. You can find the same sub-legal labor market at Lowes and Home Depot parking lots in the half-light of every dawn.

There's problem here, but it's not illegal immigration. It's an under supplied labor market, and it will only get worse over the next generation. The baby boom generation, that post-war demographic bubble, is retiring at a rate of 200,000 a month, and it takes a lot more maturing young people to replace them than it took to replace previous retirees. Because there was no corresponding spike in births 20 years ago to match this departing one (in fact birthrates have reached record lows[19]), the shortfall in replacement labor can only come from immigration. Hence the tremendous economic force drawing migrants across our southern border.

This development presents a golden political opportunity for the GOP. Since Mitt Romney's defeat in November and all the subsequent talk about the changing ethnic hue of the country's population, there has been a stream of obituaries written for what is supposed to be the white-Anglo dependent, anti-immigrant Republican Party.

But of the two major parties, the Republicans are better positioned philosophically to champion this cause. It's the party of freedom and opportunity, which is the language of immigration, not entitlement programs. Marco Rubio struck the right theme in his Jack Kemp Foundation Leadership Award speech.[20] Speaking of the waves of willing workers that we will need in this new century, he said, "Their journey is our nation's destiny. And if they can give their children what our parents gave us, the 21st-century America will be the single greatest nation that man has ever known."

We already have an immigration bottleneck. The seemingly uncontrollable flow of immigrants into our country illegally is sufficient evidence of this. To the extent we succeed in cracking down, fruit goes unpicked and roofs go unshingled.

But we need more than the tempest tossed and sweated brows. A modern economy needs tech-savvy workers, skilled specialists, and gifted entrepreneurs. Hard working men and women from Honduran villages arrive full of promise but they're unprepared to fill the positions being vacated by people who came of age in the 1960s and '70s, and our schools and homes are doing a wretched job of equipping people academically and socially to pick up the ball.

We should open immigration offices in the world's major universities, including Canadian ones, and shop for the world's brightest young people who are open to a move. As a Canadian graduate student and visa worker in the '80s and '90s, I had great difficulty staying "in status" and then getting citizenship. It always puzzled me why the government wasn't courting me to stay. Today there's even less reason for such an unwelcoming stance.

"The world must be peopled," said Shakespeare's Benedick. So too must our growing nation. Since we have chosen smaller families, we must beckon the world to hopeful shores of liberty.

A Welcoming Immigration Agenda

December 31, 2012

Last week I argued on strictly economic grounds that the United States needs to pursue an aggressive immigration agenda, not only admitting more immigrants but also actively recruiting them. But life is more than economics. Immigration policy is also a matter of national hospitality.

It's a biblical principle that when God has been good to you, you should bless others with the goods you have received. "Freely you have received, so freely give." This is true of one's home. A good home—whether from means or from cheer—is a home to be shared. Though sharing spends the means, it enriches the cheer.

Christine Pohl has written helpfully on this subject in *Making Room: Recovering Hospitality as a Christian Tradition* (Eerdmans, 1999). "Hospitality," she writes, "is a way of life fundamental to Christian identity." But she offers this caution:

> People who become known for their generous response to strangers often find increasing numbers of strangers at their door. … Sometimes, as the numbers or the frequency of guests increase, hosts find themselves stretched to their limits. Energy, resources, space, identity, and cohesion of the family or the community are strained. Faced with such pressures, host communities either work out guidelines or give up hospitality, or the community itself gradually disintegrates.

The gift of a good home, if it's to be shared, must be maintained as giftable.

The same considerations can be applied to the welcome we extend as a nation to immigrants. (I make this argument in *Left, Right, and Christ: Evangelical Faith in Politics*.) God has given us a good land and the grace to build a humane (though all too human) society on it. One of a number of ways we can share this is by opening our doors to the persecuted, the suffering, and "the huddled masses yearning to breathe free." But according to that same moral imperative, immigration though generously permitted must be controlled so we maintain the goodness of the gift to be shared. For example, the welcome must be proportional so that we don't admit so many so fast that the country the arrivals find here becomes indistinguishable from the countries they left.

It's true that nations once had open borders, but international migration was controlled by the natural limitations that the methods of communication and transportation of the day imposed. The long journey by boat in confined quarters dissuaded all but the most adventurous or desperate.

But word travels fast these days. If all the needy and the crushed from the far reaches of the globe were to flow into our nation, the good we attempt to share with "the tempest-tost" would get lost in the flood. In attempting to give to too many we would fail in our efforts and at the same time rob our neighbors, our children, and our descendants.

But love is costly and people are not morally free to escape its risks, whether privately or as a nation. Our nation's immigration policy should be faithfully and bravely hospitable. That's not just sound economics. It's also true religion.

Everybody Loves Immigration ... or Should

August 12, 2013

Ann Coulter this week tweeted, "[Bill] O'Reilly can't be that smart, he's pro-immigration." Perhaps she meant "pro-immigration reform bill" or "pro-accommodation for illegal aliens." But even so, how did we get to the point where someone who appears to be a patriotic, freedom-loving conservative could utter those words? Most Americans are pro-immigration because it's the American way.

Support for immigration itself stands at 63 percent. Forty percent are satisfied with current levels, whereas a record 23 percent advocate even higher levels. A PPP poll shows, state-to-state, 61 to 78 percent support the current immigration reform bill.

Since illegal immigration became an issue again, those on the left have rhetorically blurred the distinction between legal and illegal immigration. They tend to speak simply of "immigration." If you oppose their policies, which for the most vocal activists involve ignoring border security and instantly naturalizing 11 million stowaways with the expectation they will register as Democrats, you are against "immigration."

It would help the conversation if more conservatives would vocally support expedited and expanded legal immigration and give reasons for their support, connecting it with the cause of liberty. This would give greater credibility to their own immigration reform proposals, and they could appeal to the inclination of many Democratic-leaning ethnic communities toward the entrepreneurial advantages of liberty-oriented policies. People tend to come here for freedom and opportunity, not welfare. That's an opening for politicians who share their interest in a free country.

Immigration is not only a political opportunity but also an economic necessity on account of America's demographic problem.[21] Our fertility rate (2.08 births per woman) is not as low as Canada's (1.59) or China's (1.55), but it lags behind the replacement rate (2.1). Enough Americans have adopted the "one and done" attitude that we need immigration for an expanding economy. Otherwise, future retirees will have too few workers to pay for their Social Security and keep the economy growing while they play golf.

Activists on the evangelical left exploit vague rhetoric of their own. Their term for blanket legalization of international turnstile-hoppers is "welcoming," and if you are against it you are denounced as cruel. But if a salesman came to my door, I might welcome him into my home and hospitably offer him a seat or a drink. If he let himself in an unlocked back door or broke in through a window, I would be under no Christian obligation to show him hospitality, but rather a quick exit, regardless of his economic distress.

Most illegal aliens in America are simply honest people looking for work who cannot find it back home. Like Jean Valjean in *Les Misérables*, they break the law out of desperation. If charity were the concern, it would be more effective and less-myopic policy to work diplomatically with Mexico to liberalize its economy and free up credit so the Mexican economy can grow to match its workforce.

The common good has a way of being good for everyone.

4. Big Government

The Bureaucracy Gospel

July 27, 2011

Sitting in New York's Dag Hammarskjöld Plaza this week, I found myself in conversation with a Rwandan woman who used to work for the United Nations, though she is now an artist. She told me that she left the UN because she became sick of the bureaucracy. She asked me, "What is the problem with bureaucracy?" I paused to think, then listed four ills: It is impersonal, unresponsive, self-serving, and inefficient. That seemed to describe my artsy, former UN-worker friend's experience quite accurately.

These four ills have a lot to do with public opposition to Big Government. (I capitalize those words because Big Government is genetically related to Big Brother.) Nationwide, federal solutions to social and economic problems (Big Government) always create and perpetuate bureaucracy and its ills. Think of the Department of Education, the Department of Health and Human Services, and the Social Security Administration. These agencies have combined budgets of approximately $238 billion and employ 132,000 people. HHS administers over $700 billion, a quarter of all federal outlays, including Medicare and Medicaid payments. It is estimated that Social Security will pay out $734 billion in benefits this year.

The current federal debt crisis is driven largely by the demography of entitlements that bureaucracies like these administer. In 1940, five years after Congress established the Social Security Administration, the ratio of workers paying into the system to beneficiaries was about 159-to-1.

Because of declining birth rates and longer life expectancies, the ratio is now about 3-to-1. With the baby boom generation, that post-war bulge in the population, now entering retirement, Social Security alone (to say nothing of Medicare and Medicaid) will quickly become a program for national financial suicide. But for bureaucratic and political reasons, the program lumbers on, unresponsive to changing social conditions.

In contrast to Big Government bureaucracies, consider the fate of Borders bookstores. *National Review's* Rich Lowry has remarked on the efficiency of the market in serving the consumer (you and your neighbors) and weeding out inefficient and irrelevant businesses: "The store fell victim to the unyielding injunction of a truly creative economy: 'Adapt, or die.' It failed to keep up with evolving technology and shifting consumer preferences, and so has been forced to make way for more adept competitors."[22] But government bureaucracies hang around, doing what they've always done, long after they have stopped serving the public good, if they ever did. Notes Lowry, "If Borders were a government agency, its budget would have been fattened up during the past few years, and it'd survive in perpetuity, whatever its merits."

There will be no solution to our debt crisis until we solve the entitlement crisis. But underlying that crisis is a political conflict over Big Government and bureaucracy. One party views these as the solution to just about every human problem. The other party prefers decentralized government and grassroots solutions, though they don't always have the courage or persuasive ability to follow through on those convictions.

As Europe buckles under the weight of debt-financed social programs, America still has time to address its social dependence on government entities that are by their very nature impersonal, unresponsive, self-serving, and inefficient. But time is quickly running out.

Living Within our National Means
October 15, 2012

I once knew a fellow with seemingly no awareness of the connection between the nice things he bought on credit (condo, Corvette, Bermuda vacation) and his resulting obligation to pay those debts. Bills were an annoying intrusion on his lifestyle. Debt collectors, like panhandlers, were people he avoided.

America has a similar debt problem. Leaving aside our credit card, college, and mortgage debt, the money our government owes on our behalf from spending more than it has taken in is now more than $16 trillion. President George W. Bush inherited a debt of $5 trillion. When President Barack Obama came to office it was $10 trillion. Our national debt is now 102 percent of our gross domestic product. That puts us in the same loser league with European calamities like Ireland, Italy, and Portugal.

Carrying some debt is fine. It's a way of spreading out payment for a big-ticket item, like a house, over several or many years at a reasonable extra cost. It can also be a way of softening the impact of a sudden large and necessary expenditure like a major car repair. But debts like these are acceptable only with a detailed and manageable plan for paying them off.

But America's endless annual deficit is not to finance improvements to our national home like new highways, or onetime national emergencies like World War II. We borrow to finance the constantly expanding demands of our national lifestyle. It's like borrowing regularly against the value of your house for daily expenses while assuming and hoping that its value will ever increase.

As a nation, we are essentially "living beyond our means," and that is stealing, a violation of God's Eighth Commandment. It is theft knowingly to borrow beyond your means to repay. We are doing this when we continually expand our deficit financing knowing that it's moving us dangerously close to national insolvency. It is theft to borrow in the knowledge that someone else will be forced to pay the debt. We are doing this when we run up a bill in our generation and leave it for the next generation to pay. Spending these borrowed funds on the poor does not justify the theft. It is phony generosity to help the needy with someone else's money.

To this Eighth Commandment concern we can add leaving ourselves vulnerable to national adversaries like China by borrowing heavily from them. This endless and mushrooming debt burden also compromises our government's ability to fulfill its most basic functions like national defense.

My friend had a personal debt crisis because he was childishly irresponsible and shortsighted. As a people, we have the same problem. On top of this, our political leaders in both parties have been shrewdly buying our votes with our own money (or line of credit) and we have been naively happy to reward them. But as our debt levels enter the danger zone, it is time for us all to grow up, make sober choices about our spending priorities, and start living within our means.

The Infrastructure of Tyranny

July 23, 2013

It's only the summer of 2013, and we are already seeing presidential office seekers poking their heads out like the first buds of a political spring. On the Democratic side Hillary Clinton is planning her steps and Vice President Joe Biden envisions himself taking the baton from President Obama. As for Republicans, Ted Cruz, having only newly warmed his Senate seat from Texas, has been making friends in Iowa. It is no secret that Sen. Marco Rubio of Florida has eyes on the White House, as does New Jersey Gov. Chris Christie, and it seems we are likely to see a second run by Texas Gov. Rick Perry.

But let us keep in mind that the race for the White House is not about the candidates; it's about the country. And the most dangerous threat facing our country at this time is arguably the growing system of surveillance that is building an infrastructure for political abuse in the future.

Ever since the post-9/11 anthrax scare, the U.S. Post Service has been photographing every piece of mail that passes through its system. If I send you a letter with my return address on it, the government has a permanent record that we corresponded. Cameras are everywhere. Manhattan streets, your ATM, the gas pump, toll booths. As with the letter shots, the records remain for data mining long into the future. The National Security Agency is assembling a database of every phone call that anyone makes.[23]

Tracking terrorists and criminals has never been easier. The upside of all this is that the authorities can catch bad guys fast. The extensive camera network in London led to quick identification and apprehension of the subway bombers in 2005. Here in America, the Boston Marathon bombers were also nabbed in short order, and other plots were snuffed out in their planning stages. But this comes at the cost of treating every citizen like a suspect.

Our government is no tyranny. But we are putting in place the infrastructure, the political architecture, for potential totalitarian rule in the future. Perhaps such technology-enabled tyranny will never come, but our Founders did not design our Constitution on the assumption that everything would be fine and that our leaders would always act honorably. Just the opposite: "Enlightened statesmen will not always be at the helm" (*The Federalist Papers* No. 10). So they divided and dispersed power, provided checks and balances, and turned ambition against ambition to guard the public safety.

And we have now seen the potential for a politically ruthless administration to use the Internal Revenue Service or a regulatory agency as a political weapon against its adversaries and politically disfavored groups. There is no proof that the White House ordered the persecution of Tea Party organizations, but clearly the tools of tyranny are in place for use in the future when people may be less vigilant and leaders less restrained.

If securing ourselves against all terrorist attacks requires us to submit ourselves to the infrastructure of tyranny, then it is better to live dangerously and free than predictably secure with only the memory of freedom and dignity. This move toward tyranny has to stop. Which of our 2016 candidates will see the danger and confront it?

5. Energy and the Environment

Political Climate Science

February 25, 2010

The global warming scam has been pressed upon us with frantic alarm by everyone from Al Gore to the Climate Research Unit (CRU) at the University of East Anglia to virtually every teacher in the public school system. Life on the planet, we were told, is in mortal danger from climate change brought on by carbon emissions. The research was in, and there was a solid "consensus" in the scientific community. The only rational and morally defensible course was to empower governments everywhere to impose severe restrictions not only on manufacturing but also on every aspect of human life. Call it our own generation's "fierce urgency of now," as Martin Luther King Jr. put it with far greater justification.

Then we discovered that what we were assured was settled science as a basis for worldwide emergency measures was actually, as *National Review's* Rich Lowry put it, just "global-warming advocacy rather than dispassionate inquiry." Hackers made an embarrassing stack of CRU emails and documents public that revealed missing and erroneous data, manipulation and suppression of data, as well as what *WORLD Magazine's* Timothy Lamer called, "a pattern of groupthink and deception among influential climate scientists." One researcher in Colorado who was connected with the CRU was discovered to have lamented candidly, "The fact is that we can't account for the lack of warming at the moment and it is a travesty that we can't."[24] Yet they and their political allies were screaming at us to turn our way of life inside out and upside down on the basis of this research they claimed was as certain as the heliocentric universe.

All of this reminds us of the truth of what Francis Bacon wrote at the outset of the scientific civilization for which he argued. In the *New Organon*, his 1620 argument for a new kind of science based on the severe discipline of a patient and rigorous method, he warned against the unreliability of the human mind in investigating nature:

> The human understanding is no dry light, but receives an infusion from the will and affections; whence proceed sciences which may be called "sciences as one would." For what a man had rather were true he more readily believes. Therefore he rejects difficult things from impatience of research; sober things, because they narrow hope; the deeper things of nature, from superstition; the light of experience, from arrogance and pride, lest his mind should seem to be occupied with things mean and transitory; things not commonly believed, out of deference to the opinion of the vulgar. Numberless in short are the ways, and sometimes imperceptible, in which the affections colour and infect the understanding (Book I, aphorism 49).

We like to think of scientists as objective inquirers into the truth, without taint of personal interest or political ambition. We have long ago given up thinking of other academics this way, i.e., people in the humanities and the so-called "soft sciences," like my own, political science. But it seems that even the priests in the white lab coats share our human weaknesses, and are tempted as we are. But of course our experience with the evolutionary biologists taught us that.

The Left's Conundrum: The Environment or the Poor

July 15, 2013

There is a fossil fuel revolution underway that will make America energy independent in the near future. But the American left receives these glad tidings as a tragedy. They opposed drilling for oil in the ANWAR region of Alaska and offshore drilling on both coasts. President Obama has joined his Democratic allies in blocking the Keystone pipeline from Canada, despite environmental accommodations on the route. Under the Obama administration, leases to oil companies have decreased by 42 percent and drilling permits have decreased 37 percent, whereas crude oil production in this country has increased 14 percent over the same period.

According to Congressional Research Services, "Since 2007, natural gas production on federal lands fell by 33 percent while production on state and private lands grew by 40 percent."[25] And whereas the fracking process that releases natural gas trapped in shale rock is another bonanza for domestic energy production and a final curtain for Middle Eastern and Russian international troublemakers, the left calls it "immoral" and regards the potential environmental impact as the sole and decisive consideration in whether to allow it.[26]

But this presents the left with a conundrum and reveals where their priorities lie between the environment and the poor.

The current American energy boom is a potential relief to America's poor. It can mean lower prices at the pump and lower home heating costs. Traveling to and from work, especially places hard to access by public transit, and fighting the winter chill are matters of critical importance for lower income people, and consume a much higher portion of their income than it does for higher income groups. According to E. Calvin Beisner of the Cornwall Alliance for the Stewardship of Creation:

> Poor Americans now spend an average of 19 percent of their income on energy. States with green energy mandates have electricity rates that average 32 percent higher than states without. If you raise energy costs for everyone by 32 percent, the poor will spend about 25 percent of their income—and that, they can't afford.[27]

Abundant domestic energy sources will mean lower fuel prices for truckers (ordinary people) and in turn lower prices for everything transported by trucks, including food. Again, this constitutes a large chunk of the cost of living for people of marginal means.

Perhaps the environmental left is blinded to this dilemma by a statist confidence that the government can step in for the poor with income supplements and other generous programs. But those programs cost money and so they require increasing government revenues, and these can only come from a growing economy and a prosperous people to tax. Lower energy costs mean more wealth up and down the income ladder to tax.

If you drive away the geese, your land will be clean but there will be no eggs for the poor.

6. THE POOR

Conservatives for the Oppressed

September 14, 2011

Upon the death of England's good King Edward VI in 1553, the Scottish Reformer John Knox confessed his and his nation's sins. He saw these as related to God's sudden withdrawal of the blessing of good government. Among other items of repentance, he included "oppression and violence we have not abhorred." Conservative evangelicals in America need to abhor oppression.

"Oppression" is a word that gets tossed around a lot on the political left, often with dubious justification. But oppression is a political and economic reality. The Bible speaks of it with deep concern and quite often. The Lord "gives justice to the oppressed" (Job 36:6 NKJV). He is a "refuge" for them (Psalm 9:9). Shouldn't godly government have the same concern? To all His people in their various spheres of life He says, "Is this not the fast that I have chosen: to loose the bonds of wickedness, to undo the heavy burdens, to let the oppressed go free, and that you break every yoke" (Isaiah 58:6)?

Oppression is the inhuman use or cruel treatment of the weak and helpless by the stronger and more secure. It's the little guy getting mugged in some way by the powerful and well-connected. The left associates oppression with capitalism and with corporations in particular. Evangelicals have become active in fighting the oppression that comes from drug traffickers and sex traffickers. Gary Haugen of International Justice Mission has mobilized a generation of young evangelicals against the beastly evil of human trafficking. But cruelty and injustice may also come from a local employer, a labor union, or a government agency.

Government's job is to protect everyone's liberty, but especially those least able to protect themselves. It's often the poor who suffer oppression, though just because you're poor does not mean you're oppressed. The Bible mentions the fatherless, the widow, and the alien. But people of this sort, who are especially vulnerable to oppression, or shall we say, abuse, attract surprisingly little attention from the political class. Whether they are in the liberty-for-all wing of the Republican Party or the social justice camp of the Democratic Party, they all claim to speak for the middle class. But members of the middle class can fend for themselves. Their chief threat comes from government social and economic engineering. No one ever mentions the poor. At best they will speak of "working" people, by which they mean highly protected, unionized employees.

As the party of liberty, human dignity, and the rule of law, the Republican Party should take up the cause of the poor and the oppressed-the little guy, if you will-as the cause of all. If the weakest among us are safe and free, then we're all safe and free. And conservative evangelicals should lead the way.

The Inefficiency of Love

September 29, 2014

New York is a city of 8 million souls—55,000 of them, just over one-half of 1 percent, are homeless. But it's still a lot of people, and a lot of suffering.

God warns His people to show a special concern for the poor among them. Proverbs tells us, "Whoever oppresses a poor man insults his Maker, but he who is generous to the needy honors him" (14:31) In the story of the Good Samaritan, Jesus teaches that our special concern for the poor within the household of God does not absolve us of responsibility of the poor stranger out on the street (Luke 10:25-37).

But the poor of whom the Bible speaks are not those who do not have televisions and iPods. Job describes them as "about to perish" (Job 29:11-17). In the ancient Roman world, about 30 percent of the population lived below the subsistence level. These were the poor. Another 60 percent lived roughly at subsistence. The nobles, the patrician class, really were the 1 percent.

I took the students in my Christ and Poverty class to New York's historic rescue missions, the Bowery Mission and the New York City Rescue Mission (NYCRM). The people we saw are the biblical poor. They have nothing: no means of support, no place even to wash. Their clothes are in tatters. Underwear is a precious gift. They are wholly unprepared to seek, secure, and hold a job. Sadly, almost all of them are alcoholics, drug addicts, or mentally ill. For the addicts and drunks, some sort of despair led them into their downward spiral of self-destruction. For all of them, something broke their connection with family. Everyone was once someone's baby.

These rescue missions have been doing great work for 140 years. NYCRM serves meals to 300 people a day and has 240 beds for nightly refuge. Both missions strive to provide "the very best for the very least," treating the guests with love and respecting their dignity, which, outside those walls, is rubbed raw. They also have, in addition to Bible studies, classes for computer skills and job hunting, and nice donated suits for the interview stage. But only a handful gets that far.

One may question the return on investment in doing so little for so few in a sea of need. These missions come nowhere close to solving New York's poverty problem. But Jesus did not command His people to "solve the poverty problem." He said to show mercy to the helpless who are in desperate need:

> I was hungry and you gave me food, I was thirsty and you gave me drink, I was a stranger and you welcomed me, I was naked and you clothed me, I was sick and you visited me, I was in prison and you came to me. (Matthew 25:35-36)

People are complicated. It takes a generation and a small fortune for a mom and dad to raise a child from infancy to adulthood, to shelter and feed, to educate, to train in the habits of hard work and charity. Any attempt to expand the scale and efficiency of this process through community day care and industrial schooling falls miserably short. So why should anyone expect that restoring adults from shattered lives and tragically disfigured hearts, even with the saving grace of God assisting as it does with our children, could be accomplished "efficiently" with a "modern" system of social services. It's face-to-face and hand-to-hand in Jesus' name. It's draining. It's often disheartening, even heartbreaking. But there is no other way.

Freedom Feeds the Poor

June 17, 2013

Jesus said, "For you always have the poor with you" (Mark 14:7). But presidents and would-be presidents like to promise otherwise. Granted, we needn't have so many of them and they needn't be so extremely poor, and love of neighbor calls us to relieve their poverty as best we can.

Since Barack Obama first ran for the presidency in 2008, he has stated that our sluggish economy and those suffering from it are his highest concern. But despite unnaturally low interest rates, various government-financed stimuli, and massive healthcare reform, the American economy continues to stumble and sputter. Our unemployment rate is officially 7.6 percent (2013), but the broader employment rate, including the underemployed and those who have given up, is 13.8 percent. But why is it so hard to get this productive country with its enormous natural resources, including a now booming domestic energy sector, into gear for our willing labor force?

Machiavelli observed, "It is a very natural and ordinary thing to desire to acquire." But you don't have to be the Renaissance teacher of evil to see this. God's eighth commandment is "You shall not steal." Ownership is good, so the desire to prosper oneself need not be evil. God also gave us a propensity to work. He commissioned us at the creation to "take dominion over the earth" (Genesis 1:26). Even His call to periodic rest came with the injunction, "six days shall you labor" (Exodus 20:9). Productive work and security in its fruits is essential to healthy human life.

So it should not surprise us to hear that when governments from South Africa to China turned from wealth redistribution to private wealth creation through private property, free markets, and free trade, productivity replaced extreme poverty at stunning rates.

Between 1990 and 2010, global extreme poverty fell by half from 43 percent of total population in developing nations to 21 percent. A billion people crossed the international extreme poverty line of $1.25 a day, beating the United Nations millennial development goals target date by five years.

This change did not result from international aid, which tends to retard economies, but from economic growth. Most of it occurred in China, which has been liberalizing its economy for more than 30 years. China's economic growth these last 10 years has ranged between 9 percent in 2011 and 14 percent in 2007. (By comparison, the U.S. economy grew 2 percent in those same years.) Between 1980 and 2010, China reduced its extreme poverty from 84 percent to 10 percent of its population. In countries with greater political equality, the benefits of economic expansion were shared more broadly across society.

By global standards, there is no "extreme poverty" in America, but there is poverty. About 22 million Americans—15 percent of the country—are receiving food stamps. It is said that one-in-six Americans are in poverty. But the lesson from abroad, a lesson we used to teach the world, is that the rising tide of freedom-fueled prosperity lifts all boats. But as stunning as this record from developing nations is, it is not stunning enough for the current administration.

The Cruelty of Minimum Wage Kindness

April 4, 2016

It is high tide for egalitarian moral passion on the political left these days. After seven years of the "hope and change" president, the dream candidate of progressive government, his supporters are seeing a crisis of material inequality. From Occupy Wall Street to the groundswell of enthusiasm for Bernie Sanders, people of a socialistic sentiment are demanding that we raise America's economic floor.

The sentiment is understandable. It is disconcerting to see some people doing so well—hedge fund managers and

Justin Bieber—while others see their purchasing power fall year after year. So California passed a minimum wage increase to $15 over the next six years. Take that, inequality! Shouldn't a Christian, or Christian-influenced, people show kindness to their neighbors by legally extending prosperity to some of the least among us?

But kindness that isn't wisely directed is cruel. A legally mandated wage increase at the bottom of the wage scale will trigger demands for increases all the way up the chain. People previously making $15 and feeling good about it will be effectively reduced to minimum wage, so they will demand, say, $21. And so on up. With more money chasing the same goods, prices will increase accordingly, and then, in real terms, the minimum wage will be back where it was before: $15 will buy what $9 used to buy.

In pushing for a higher minimum wage in New York where the law requires $9 an hour, Gov. Andrew Cuomo said, "You cannot raise a family, pay for rent and food and insurance and healthcare on $18,000 a year in the city of New York." But to pay for all of that in metro New York you need at least $60,000, or $30 an hour plus benefits. A decent family income is not the point of the $9 wage, however. It is for entry-level work, low-skilled labor, and part-time employment. People who want a higher wage need to improve their skills or their marketability in some other way, not lobby the government to force more money out of employers.

I know a waitress who is very unhappy that New York raised the minimum wage for tipped workers from $5 an hour to $7.50. The premise of the lower wage is that these workers make the bulk of their income in tips. For restaurant owners, the wage hike is a 50 percent increase in labor costs, which are one-third of overall operating costs.

So the immediate result for wait staff is layoffs or fewer hours and more tables to serve. This reduces the quality of service, resulting in lower tips. I have seen this happen. Higher prices from higher labor costs also disincline people to tip. As people become aware that table servers are paid more, they will feel less pressure to tip because the compensation is thought to be, as it were, baked into the cost of the meal. That waitress' message to her friends in government is: Keep your helping hands to yourself!

As it is always with well-meaning misuses of government, the poor suffer while the rich feel good about themselves. Government is a clumsy, blunt instrument, useful mostly for punishing evildoers and repelling invaders. Charity is best left to the good judgment of neighbors. If there's a problem with that, then average citizen character is something we need to work on anyway.

You Can Be Replaced

May 12, 2014

Machines are putting people out of work. You'll notice there are no more elevator operators. You push your own button, and the thing moves. And when you place a telephone call, voice contact with a telephone operator is gone. And where's the guy who pumps your gas, checks your oil, and cleans your windshield? Also gone! It's a wonder anyone is working at all.

I was born when John F. Kennedy was president, so I don't remember any of these services. But I do remember when bank machines came into use in the 1980s. Automated tellers. Of course, I was all over them. But now I prefer the human touch inside my community bank where my face is a valid form of identification. Behind wickets there are still real people who can take my check and count out my cash and who I can call by name.

I'm less interested in the human touch at the post office. It's gruff and rude. But that's just the particular humans at my post office. I do prefer to swipe my credit card at gas stations and get back on the road. Perhaps it's also a feature of Big Store suburban life that I find it a net gain to use the automated cashier at places like Home Depot and supermarkets. They give you that choice.

Cashiers at McDonald's restaurants who are fussing for a raise from the $7.25 minimum wage to $15 should remember this brief history and their own experience with automated services. I've seen people striking in front of the Golden Arches in T-shirts that read, "We're Worth More." Well, McDonald's may find that while these people themselves are priceless, the services they provide are not worth anything close to $15 an hour. The cost of their labor will not have to rise much before machines become more cost effective for the company. You can even program these machines to smile and exchange pleasantries. When that happens, it will be no more lamentable than the disappearance of elevator operators and the advent of EZPass lanes at toll plazas that cut the number of attendants who are paid enormous salaries to give you change for a five.

So what about all the folks who will no longer have those particular low skill jobs? The policy question is not how to keep those jobs, much less how to inflate their wages beyond what their minimal skills are worth. The question is how to cultivate a population that more widely has the sort of life and work skills that command higher wages. That has to begin with an honest and effective family policy.

On the other end of things, the further exclusion of cash from our economy means that retailers will be that much more able to track our spending habits and in turn influence them for their advantage, not necessarily ours.

7. Gun Control

The Hunting Amendment?
January 21, 2013

In the wake of massacre of schoolchildren in Newtown, Conn., the movie theatre shootings in Aurora, Colo., and a string of similar incidents too long to ignore, a growing number of people are alarmed at the attachment so many of their fellow countrymen have to owning military-style assault rifles with large capacity ammunition clips. "You can't use those for hunting," they say. "I've never seen a deer with a bullet proof vest!" They add, "People can certainly own hunting rifles or handguns to protect their homes, but there's no reason for anyone to own battlefield weaponry."

I am more alarmed at why so many supposedly informed members of the commentary class think that our Founding Fathers passed the Second Amendment—clearly a high national priority right behind the freedoms of speech and religion—to protect the freedom to hunt, practice marksmanship, or guard against home invaders.

The Second Amendment reads:

> "A well regulated Militia, being necessary to the security of a free State, the right of the people to keep and bear Arms, shall not be infringed."

Like the protections of the First Amendment, such as for speech and the press, the right to bear arms has a specifically political purpose. State militias and privately armed citizens are an extra layer of security against foreign invasion, i.e., they help keep a "free State." Article 1, Section 8 of the Constitution provides for Congress calling up the militia "to execute the Laws of the Union, suppress Insurrections and repel Invasions."

One of the reasons no one invaded Switzerland in the 20th century, aside from their imposing geography, is the widely armed citizenry that is trained for militia service.

But a government can just as easily take away its country's freedom. The Founders did not want the federal government controlling a large standing army because they were wary of creating a large, powerful, tyrannical government in the nation's capital, far removed from the people. So they foresaw national defense resting largely on federal use of state militias, and that only on American soil. Though Congress may "raise and support Armies," funding for their use is constitutionally limited to two-year appropriations.

Though the Constitution provides for federal use of state militias to "suppress insurrection," the Founders must have feared the possibility of an increasingly tyrannical government expanding its armies and disbanding potential armed opposition at the state level. For this reason, they added the Second Amendment. Armed citizens are a bulwark against national tyranny.

On this understanding, the people's right to own weapons that are designed for specifically military use is what the Constitution protects. And if it protects these weapons, it also protects all lesser grade firearms, like hunting rifles, shotguns, and handguns.

People are free to think what they want about this provision: absurdly outdated, or even ill-conceived from the start. But it's the fundamental law of the land. We may amend it, but we may not ignore it or "interpret" it away as merely "the hunting amendment."

Another Mass Shooting

October 5, 2015

It was a couple of days before we could piece together the details surrounding the mass shooting at Umpqua Community College in Roseburg, Oregon: the shooter's identity; his background, motives, and mental health; the number and names of the slain and wounded; and the murder weapons and how the killer obtained them. But it was just a few hours after the first shots that President Obama was scolding the nation with his fatherly displeasure over our unwillingness to support stricter gun control laws.

He expressed the puzzled anger that many of us feel: "Somehow this has become routine." But for Obama, the "somehow" is not a question. He believes Americans frequently massacre each other because our easy access to guns, unique in the industrialized world (if you ignore Switzerland), allows it. If we tighten gun access, he says, we will disarm the mentally ill and the emotionally disturbed "angry young men."

But the "somehow" is much more complicated. Why are these mass murderers largely white young men? Why these white young men? Why now and not 50 years ago? We have always had guns but we have not always had gun massacres. What kind of family lives, community lives, and religious lives did these killers have? Is there a significant pattern in their mental health or criminal or disciplinary records? How many of them used illegally obtained weapons or did not personally own their weapons? How many used handguns or rifles, automatic or semi-automatic guns? How many incidents occurred in states with strict gun control laws or in "gun-free zones"?

If we ban guns, will killers bent on slaughter use explosives? The Columbine killers came prepared with a 20-pound propane bomb, and the Colorado cinema killer rigged his apartment with homemade devices.

After the UC Santa Barbara killings, Obama expressed his frustration that society was not willing to take the "basic steps to keep guns out of the hands of people who can do just unbelievable damage." But identifying those sociopathic needles in the national haystack is impossible short of total-itarian government control. They look a lot like hay. The president's dry-up-the-guns approach would require a New York City—style virtual ban on legal gun ownership, as in the massacre-free countries that Obama recommended for our consideration.

What strikes me in this sad regularity of public shootings is not any generic gun violence but the extremely unstable people who want to kill crowds of strangers. Whether it is by guns (legal or illegal), knives, or explosives is secondary. W. Bradford Wilcox at *National Review* sees a pattern of fatherless homes among these killers: divorces, absent fathers, and mothers never having married. That's something to consider before depriving law-abiding Americans of their right to self-defense.[28]

Political leaders would be wiser to focus on the family, to make a habit of examining more closely the nation's laws and policies for their effect on that cradle of character, community, and religion. Even marginally good families are much less likely to produce isolated, angry, murderous young men and much more likely to intervene successfully in ways that are impossible for a government of a free people.

Rounding Up the Guns
October 19, 2015

It's alarming that Hillary Clinton has expressed openness to a mandatory gun buyback program modeled on an Australian one that President Obama referenced in his remarks about the Umpqua Community College shooting in Oregon. In response to a question from the audience at a campaign stop, Clinton said, "I think it would be worth considering doing it on a national level, if that could be arranged."

But in America, such a gun purge is neither possible nor desirable.

As to the feasibility, there are 350 million guns in private American possession, 10 million of which are the semi-automatic, so-called military-style AR-15s. Our Constitution's Second Amendment guarantees the right "to keep and bear arms," and repealing the amendment is politically inconceivable at this time. Partly because of this legal guarantee and partly because of our frontier heritage, we have always had a deeply rooted gun culture. To impose a national program of gun confiscation on such a people would be an intolerable act of tyranny.

A move to round up all the legally owned guns in the country is also undesirable. People have a natural right to defend themselves against criminal violence. This summer, convicted murderers Richard Matt and David Sweat escaped from prison in upstate New York. These were cold-blooded, merciless killers. No one had any reliable idea where they were. They could have been heading westward to Matt's native Buffalo. Perhaps they were making their way north to the Canadian border. They could have been in anyone's woodshed. People had guns on their kitchen tables and at their bedsides because anything could have happened at any time, and the police can't be everywhere. New Yorkers were glad for their guns. People feel the same way in many under-policed, crime-saturated neighborhoods across the country.

But are gun rights even Christian? Does God expect His faithful ones to testify to our hope in what we cannot lose—our eternal lives—by letting home invaders and mass killers take what we cannot keep—our earthly lives? Jesus warns, "All who take the sword will perish by the sword" (Matthew 26:52). But He tells the disciples whom He sends out in his name to buy swords for their journeys (Luke 22:36). Jesus tells His people not to resist people who do us evil, but instead to turn the other cheek when they are assaulted (Matthew 5:39). But His examples are of those who strike us or rob us, not try to kill us. When someone strikes a man's wife, his Christian obligation is not to turn her other cheek but to defend her as appropriate. So too one's home, one's fellow worshipers, or one's neighbors at the convenience store or on campus.

8. RACE AND POLICE

The Police Problem

August 18 and December 8, 2014

When I was a boy, they told us in school that a policeman is your friend. There are communities where that does not appear to be true. Those communities also tend to be especially troubled by crime. That complicates the relationship. Ferguson, Mo., seems to have one of those complicated policing relationships.

This northern suburb of St. Louis has had a high crime rate, but not everyone in Ferguson is a criminal—far from it. Not even most young people. Aggressive policing has reduced the crime rate but increased tensions within the community, as people walking on the right side of the law get swept up at times with the outlaws.

After the Michael Brown shooting, resentment burst into the streets in protest, unintentionally providing cover for the criminal element to loot. The police then responded with a stance and presence more suited to the Battle of Fallujah. There is no conceivable reason a sniper should be posted on top of an armored vehicle on an American street. A local police force equipped with arms designed for fighting foreign wars becomes more of a threat to public safety than a protection.

The police problem is an expression of "the political problem" to which James Madison gave the clearest statement in *The Federalist Papers* No. 51:

> In framing a government which is to be administered by men over men, the great difficulty lies in this: you must first enable the government to control the governed; and in the next place oblige it to control itself.

Political authority takes different forms and so too does the problem: self-serving political leaders and bureaucracies, abusive police forces, armies that pillage instead of defend.

There are dangerous people among us, so we need uniformed people authorized to arrest and incarcerate, and even to use deadly force, if necessary, to protect the peace. If the police were simply a force for evil, we could just remove them. No problem. But if the police withdrew for the sake of peace, there would be mayhem. Despite abuses, every police force provides an essential service. Police officers deserve gratitude, no matter how mixed it may be, from the communities they serve.

A police force, though necessary, is dangerous. The power

to protect is also the power to assault. So the police themselves can become a threat. Police work attracts a particular kind of person: virile, combative, eager to face a challenge. The job demands this. But to keep those qualities serving the public good, we train officers in self-control and professional conduct, and we constrain them with policies that help everyone involved. And we subject them also to elected political oversight. In Ferguson, the police chief answers to the mayor who in turn answers to the voters.

Police officers are trained to deal professionally with intense conflict and stressful situations. But they have their human limits. The mayor of Ferguson tried to elicit sympathy for everyone involved when he reflected,

> I am confident that all the law enforcement agencies that are participating are professionals, and if there [are] some videos that show someone losing their temper in a highly stressful situation, I'm sure they're under a great deal of stress and though it does not make it okay, they are human and I can understand their frustrations as well. Just as the protesters are frustrated.

When a law enforcement officer has to deal regularly with vicious sociopaths (there are some in every community, in some more than others), it is tempting for him to view the whole community as an enemy, especially if the community is not his community, is ethnically homogenous, and not his ethnicity.

For the community's part, rage is never constructive. "Love builds up" (1 Cor. 8:1). God solved the basic human problem through his love for us on the cross. Loving one's enemy, whether real or perceived, is far from easy, as the life of Rev. John Perkins illustrates.[29] James, the brother of Jesus, wrote, "Let every person be quick to hear, slow to speak, slow to anger; for the anger of man does not produce the righteousness of God" (James 1:19—20). Honest, humble, empathetic listening between residents and police, taking seriously each other's concerns, would at least be a step forward.

The political, economic, and social situation in Ferguson is extremely complicated and its interpreters should resist easy explanations like poverty or racism. Human government is difficult. Trust is fragile. Statesmanship is rare. This is why we pray for all those in authority, "that we may lead a peaceful and quiet life, godly and dignified in every way" (1 Timothy 2:1—2).

Police Protests Have Consequences

January 5, 2015

There should have been nothing remarkable in Carson Daly sporting a NYPD cap for hosting the NBC New Year's Eve coverage from Times Square. It was New York City after all, and New York's finest were keeping everyone safe in the target of choice for jihadist terrorists. But he sparked a Twitter storm of praise and vile cursing. Such is the mood.

Since a St. Louis grand jury declined to bring charges in the shooting death of Michael Brown and after a year of racial tensions,[30] there have been continuous demonstrations against what some claim is local police racism. But these organized and sustained demonstrations of anti-police invective have emboldened the morally unstable to attack the police who protect every community. Seeking redress for what they claim is injustice, they are endangering everyone.

One march chanted, "What do we want? Dead cops!" On another occasion, a small communist group shouted "Stand up, shoot back." So it is no surprise that people are boldly threatening the police on social media and to their faces. We also have seen an unusual willingness of some to resist arrest. A Brooklyn man sent an officer to the hospital from a blow to the face. In Boston, seven teenagers beat and choked officers attempting to apprehend someone who skipped his court date. Worst of all, a career criminal assassinated two New York police officers in broad daylight as they were sitting in their cruiser.

This climate has also led New York City police to pull back from confronting minor incidents. The opposite of the "broken windows" theory of policing,[31] it will allow a culture of law-breaking to provide deeper soil for more serious criminality. This is also related to Mayor Bill de Blasio undermining his own police force by expressing fears for his biracial son after the Eric Garner grand jury decision. In so doing, he emboldened the vilification of police and violent assaults on them by the lawless fringe. Actions have consequences.

It is a mark of adult behavior to consider the consequences of one's actions before launching them. The police consider that a matter of professional discipline. When judgment fails them, they are held responsible. The Boston police officers who were injured in the teen attack chose to use pepper spray and suffer injury instead of pulling their guns, even though, had they been overcome in the melee, they could have lost their guns and then their lives.

Protests also have consequences—for their speech, their tone, their duration, and the company and conduct they tolerate. In Ferguson, Mo., they would have had more credibility had they taken steps against looters. In New York, they would have been wise to heed requests for a day of silent respect as the slain offers were buried, or at least carried signs saying "We love good cops" and maybe donned NYPD caps of their own.

9. Family

The Family Crisis

February 24, 2012

Our nation is in a crisis. Yes, all eyes are on the financial crisis and the stagnant economy, and less certain but potentially ominous is the prospect of a nuclear-armed and religiously fanatical Iran. But it is possible that we might revive the economy at home and disarm our enemies abroad while losing the nation itself. I'm talking about the disintegration of the family that is quietly reaching crisis proportions.

In 2012, Marvin Olasky drew attention to a tipping point we have passed in single parenthood. "For the first time in American history, more than half (53%) of all births to American women under 30 are occurring outside of marriage."[32] The Heritage Foundation reports that, of all births in the United States, 41% are out of wedlock. That figure is 53% in France, but only 32% in Canada.

This is not just a matter of "the times they are a-changing." The family is the foundation of society on which all other goods ultimately depend. It is in the family that children are formed into psychologically stable, morally self-controlled, economically productive, and politically public-spirited adults. Incidentally, it is also in the family where covenant children are discipled into faithful Christians. It is not impossible for socially functional and Christ-confessing adults to emerge from broken families, but studies show consistently that it is a lot less likely. In neighborhoods where fathers are a rarity, poverty, unemployment, and crime are dramatically higher, and high school graduation dramatically lower, than in communities of largely intact families.

In 2011, Chuck Donovan at The Heritage Foundation called for "A Marshall Plan for Marriage." He writes, "This breakdown of the American family has dire implications for American society and the U.S. economy. Halting and reversing the sustained trends of nearly four decades will not happen by accident." Governments need to identify this increasingly widespread pattern of behavior as a serious threat to our national security. Echoing the Reagan administration's 1983 report on American schooling, "A Nation at Risk," one could justly say that if an unfriendly foreign power attempted to impose on America the family patterns that exist today, we might well view it as an act of war.

To combat this multi-generational trend (or what Olasky calls "an ooze, a sociological horror film that could be titled The Blob That Ate America"), Donovan recommends that every level of government eliminate discouragements to marriage in the tax code and welfare programs, maximize the reconciliation option for divorcing couples, and encourage and support family life by the way government leaders and bureaucracies talk about marriage and family and by the way they present their program goals.

In times of crisis, we need statesmen who see what is most important and know what we need to do about it, and who have the moral stature and gifts of leadership that it takes to wed the rest of us with requisite passion to these goals and measures. President Obama has a nice family. If he were to take up this cause with energy and understanding, he could become a great president in his second term. Sadly, he seems too committed to advancing the causes of the problem, such as the paternalistic welfare state, to appreciate the nature of the problem and its remedies.

Abortion and the Modern People We Are

August 10, 2015

It is not often that people both across the country and in the media are shocked and sickened by the practices of a liberal darling organization like Planned Parenthood. Nonetheless, its national president, Cecile Richards, was defiant and many of its prominent supporters stood up for the nation's largest abortion provider, including the White House and Hillary Clinton, the 2016 Democratic presidential front-runner. Harvesting the intact body parts of aborted babies and selling them is not an unfortunate departure from the modern world's march of progress; it's what happens when scientific civilization divorces Christian civilization and becomes a technologically empowered cult of selfish autonomy.

Modern people expect to control the world—it's what modern means. The world is chaotic and dangerous and needs taming to make it predictable and safe, and modern science provides that. Through a disciplined method of discovery based on a new way of looking at the world, modern inventions have flowed like a river with an ever-wider and stronger current. But the blessings have been mixed. The internet's information revolution and rapid email communication also brought a deluge of pornography and shattered spans of attention. Breathtaking medical advances arrived hand-in-hand with germ warfare and "safe," clinical abortion.

This modern project to make us masters of the universe looks a lot like taking "dominion over the earth" in obedience to God's command in Genesis 1:26. But that requires seeing ourselves as God's image-bearers in God's world under God's authority for God's purposes. Without that, we are left with tyrannical domination with no moral guidance but our selfish desires.

In *The Abolition of Man*, C. S. Lewis warned that man's control of nature necessarily becomes the power of some people over most people. And as reason is no longer understood to be for hearing and understanding God but only for conquering nature and calculating our personal advantage in using it, nature paradoxically reassumes control since only the passions are left, most often the selfish ones, to guide our use of that power.

The abortion gospel is all about empowering those passions. In 2008, presidential candidate Barack Obama defended abortion rights as being necessary to "ensure that our daughters have the same rights, freedoms, and opportunities [control] as our sons to fulfill their dreams [selfish desires]." For women to share equally with men in modern personal autonomy—unconstrained by God, morality, or nature—they must have free access to abortion, even, if necessary, as the baby is being born.

Agents of Planned Parenthood who haggle over a baby-part price list like they're selling old housewares at a yard sale are simply acting as modern people who believe the world is stuff to be subdued and transformed for servicing their desires. The sobering truth is that modern Christians share in this morally and spiritually unrestrained drive to conquer the world technologically for our comfort and convenience. The prophet Daniel confessed that the sins of his people were his own sins too (Daniel 9:4-11). Where are we guilty of pursuing our selfish autonomy with implicit indifference to God's authority and purposes?

10. The Sexual Revolution

The Long Road to Same-sex Marriage

July 1, 2013

I am not surprised at the U.S. Supreme Court decision, *Hollingsworth v. Perry*, which struck down the 1996 Defense of Marriage Act (DOMA) and affirmed homosexual rights. Popular support for same-sex marriage is at 53 percent, up from 30 percent in 2004. Writing for the majority and emboldened by these polls, Justice Anthony Kennedy went beyond returning the question to the states. He gratuitously vilified advocates of traditional marriage, asserting that the only basis for opposing same-sex marriage is a "bare congressional desire to harm a politically unpopular group," i.e., malice. He was feeling the moral high ground.

But this is the culmination of a centuries-old moral and political trajectory. America was founded on a synthesis of Christianity and 17th century Enlightenment philosophy. The Enlightenment thought of John Locke and friends is individualist and politically minimalist. In this view, we are fundamentally autonomous individuals, and our only moral obligation is not to violate one another's life, liberty, or property unless one's own security requires it. We are not God's image-bearers, called to embody God's entire moral law as Christ did.

The moral heritage of historic Christianity has long restrained the radical individualism of this political theory, albeit with varying degrees of success and of fidelity to the Scriptures. But by fits and starts, we have fallen away from not only Christian faith and church involvement, but also the cultural dividend that has helped sustain us as faith and religion waned. "Compassion," a politically appealing word, would have no moral weight among us were it not for the now thinning cultural atmosphere of Christian civilization. The word gets no mention in *Aristotle's Ethics*, and there would be no Red Crescent if there had been no Red Cross.

We are left increasingly with just autonomous, egalitarian individualism. (Our statism grows out of our individualism as de Tocqueville explains in *Democracy in America*.) Thus advocates of same-sex marriage frame the issue as "marriage equality." They are no threat to life, liberty, or property, so there can be no valid moral objections. President Barack Obama, who opposed it in 2008, recently made the same morally indifferent egalitarian appeal for same-sex marriage: "We are all created equal, and the love we commit to one another must be equal as well." Love is love.

Society is reduced to an association of mere human-being-units who desire and choose. We see it in the brutal selfishness of ever-widening abortion rights, the feminist interchangeability of men and women even in frontline military combat, and the reduction of marriage to a kind of institutionalized sexual indulgence with no inherent connection to children as the natural fruit of the relationship and the protected beneficiaries of the institution itself.

This cultural plunge into marriage chaos is not primarily the fault of "those people" stealing our country. Fault lies with the church's 250-year failure, on balance, to guard biblical doctrine and disciple covenant children faithfully. Same-sex marriage is a symptom, not the disease.

How We Dug Our Way Down the Rabbit Hole

May 11, 2015

A *Wall Street Journal/NBC News* poll reveals that support for same-sex marriage in the United States has reached 59 percent, and that more people would be comfortable with a homosexual president than with an evangelical one. We are witnessing the collapse of what is left of the Christian moral consensus, with stunningly swift reversals on sexuality, personal identity, and marriage. How did we get here?

It's complicated. But for 250 years, American Protestant Christians have dwelt all too comfortably with modern individualism, which has inclined them to a default position of Arminian, Baptistic, and more or less independent churches. My free will—my freedom to steer the course of my life—is understood to be a principle before which even God Himself bows in reverence. In other words, "don't fence me in" applied to religion.

This attitude replaced a covenantal view that sees God, not man, as the center and primary mover of human affairs. Consider the once commonly used phrase, "There but for the grace of God go I," Abraham Lincoln's assurance in his second inaugural address that "The Almighty has His own purposes," and the reference in the Declaration of Independence to "a firm reliance on the protection of divine providence."

Accordingly, in the broader culture (the culture that was raised in the church and departed from it), to be most human is to be most unconstrained, whether by tradition, nature, or God. Justice Anthony Kennedy wrote in the 1992 abortion case *Planned Parenthood v. Casey*, "At the heart of liberty is the right to define one's own concept of existence, of meaning, of the universe, and of the mystery of human life." Most ninth graders would agree with this.

So American churches generally do not hold their members spiritually accountable. They do not "discipline" them. In non-denominational churches there is often no formal membership at all. The customer wants to be in control, and the religious service provider is happy to accommodate.

But that individualistic understanding, nurtured in part by a uniquely modern and characteristically American strain of Christianity, is bearing us along to the absurdity of its logical outworking. If we are essentially autonomous individuals, everyone's fundamental obligation is to respect each other's individual self-determination. This side of the sexual revolution, sex is no big deal but at the same time definitive of who you are, something that, of course, should be within your personal control. After the complete triumph of feminism, sexual differences mean something only when we want them to. So it is no surprise that people are not only tolerating but celebrating homosexual marriage and the very notion of definable or even distinguishable "he" and "she" is officially unacceptable. People and organizations that think otherwise disqualify themselves from civil protections.

Heresy is always an opportunity for the church to refine her beliefs in light of biblical teaching. American Christians need to acknowledge our complicity in this rebellion against God's created order and resolve to re-examine biblical faithfulness in a hostile world.

Sex and the City of Man

November 9, 2015

Christians, as citizens of the kingdom of God, are wrestling with how to live as citizens of progressive America. Michael Gerson and Peter Wehner, both of whom served in the George W. Bush administration, offer their counsel on "How Christians Can Flourish in a Same-Sex Marriage World." In their *Christianity Today* cover story, the co-authors of *City of Man: Religion and Politics in a New Era* (Moody, 2010) reject either "calling a crusade or taking a sabbatical" and viewing America as either "a moral cesspool or the Babylon of Christian exile."

The same-sex marriage defeat, they say, dates back a half century to changes in marriage law and the sexual revolution, so reversing it will take the multi-generational witness of faithful Christian families. True. They suggest we "leverage this moment" with "a new model of social engagement." We'll have to defend our religious liberty, but if all we do is defend ourselves we will become merely another aggrieved minority. To earn our neighbors' attention and admiration we have to focus on "the priority of humans"—their rights, well being, and dignity—everyone from the unborn to the poor and incarcerated to the many victims of the sexual revolution.

Good. But Gerson and Wehner too easily dismiss the importance of what we do sexually and how we understand ourselves in that doing. "When it comes to cultural analysis," they say, "many evangelicals have sex too much on their minds." They cite C. S. Lewis on the greater danger of sins that are solely of the spirit, like self-righteousness and vindictiveness.

But the sexual revolution is not just about the licentious freedom to follow our impulses among consenting adults. It is a radical revisioning of what a human being is, namely, a sophisticated beast that is radically autonomous, even self-creating, in a godless universe. Thus, we don't receive or discover our moral framework. We simply will whatever morality we fancy. We will even ourselves, our identity. So, for example, children are not born boy or girl, but rather at some time choose to identify as one or the other. There is no sovereign Creator-God, only sovereignty over oneself and thus sexual autonomy.

And that's why so-called progressives are keen on a sexually libertine culture, especially on college campuses, with unrestricted access to abortion, liberal divorce laws, redefinition of marriage to the point of its disappearance, and now transgender rights. The sexual dimension of the culture wars is not ultimately about "sins of the flesh" but about what it means to be human. If Christians don't speak up on this matter, there is almost no one else who will. It is hard to speak in defense of people's humanity when the very concept of "human" is in flux.

If Christians do not clearly articulate for themselves—not only in church but also in the public square—how the sexual revolution is evil, self-destructive for everyone who embraces it, and corrosive to all their relationships, it will continue to poison the church and cripple her ability to worship God, love neighbor, and pass on the faith from generation to generation.

Our Transgendered Future

June 30, 2014

You are hateful and on the wrong side of history. You just don't know it yet. Today's normal is tomorrow's appalling prejudice.

Take this: Christin Scarlett Milloy wrote a startling piece at *Slate.com*, "Don't Let Your Doctor Do This To Your Newborn," about that point after delivery when the doctor identifies the sex of the baby, speaking as if it were a creepy, dangerous, and controversial procedure:

> It's called infant gender assignment: When the doctor holds your child up to the harsh light of the delivery room, looks between its legs, and declares his opinion: It's a boy or a girl, based on nothing more than a cursory assessment of your offspring's genitals.

The article is a rhetorical attempt to mold your thinking into the way so-called "transgender" people see the world, and to bring you to see yourself, your children, and everyone that way. Now that homosexuality has been completely normalized and the nationalization of same-sex marriage is proceeding swiftly, transgender rights and accommodations are the next cultural battlefront.[33]

Transgender is the T in LGBT (lesbian, gay, bisexual, and transgender). The term assumes a distinction between sex and gender. Whereas ordinarily these words are synonymous, activists for this cause claim that whereas anatomy and chromosomes determine sex, gender pertains to how one identifies and feels about oneself. So though a baby is born, for example, female, its gender—whether boy or girl—is yet to emerge or be chosen. Or so they say.

By using these terms repeatedly in this way and by appealling to the language of rights, the sanctity of choice and the priority of personal autonomy, they will carry the day.

This will affect you. There is a logic and a pattern of cultural conquest that these causes follow. California schools have already established a legal right for students to "self-identify" as a boy or a girl and play on corresponding sports teams, giving "transgender kindergarten-through-12th grade students … access to whichever restroom and locker room they want."

Next, men who feel they are women will be allowed to use women's restrooms. Then all restrooms will just become unisex. How you feel about that as a fellow restroom patron doesn't matter. You need to get over your archaic feelings of discomfort.

Hospitals and professional associations will start disciplining doctors who announce "It's a boy!" or "It's a girl!"

Schools will stop registering children as either boy or girl. The system will take "gender identity" as indeterminate until teachers have explained the issue, presented all available options, and received the child's deliberate choice. If too many children choose the gender "traditionally" associated with their physiology, the school will assume it has failed to make the options and the freedom to choose sufficiently clear. The politically favored pressure groups will accept nothing less. Progressive and conflict-averse administrators will follow this course aggressively.

Anyone who is not actively sensitive to this concern will be viewed as a public enemy, even as people are now viewed who indicate moral disagreement with homosexual behavior.

The upside could be that Christians come to see their distinct difference as Christ's church more clearly, determine to live more circumspectly and faithfully, love their enemies more intentionally, and suffer more cheerfully. We could get more serious with that right away.

The New Politics of Identity

December 28, 2015

It's a mad, mad, mad world and getting madder. Mark Twain once quipped, "Common sense is very uncommon," and it's less common today than ever before. The difference between The Onion, that ridiculous online fount of satire, and a serious news source is becoming ever more difficult to discern.

When I first read that a 52-year-old married father of seven in Toronto had not only declared himself transgendered but was self-identifying as a 6-year-old girl, I thought it was a joke, a *reductio ad absurdum* mockery of current leftist orthodoxies. But no!

Paul Wolscht now goes by the name "Stefonknee." He even has adoptive "parents." And why not? If homosexuals can "marry," if a person can "self-identify" as the opposite sex despite all anatomical evidence to the contrary, and if the former president of the Spokane chapter of the NAACP and oh-so-white Rachel Dolezal can "self-identify" as black, then why can't this fellow require you to accept him as a little girl?

But if we honor his radically free will and personal autonomy in this way, is he required to have legal guardians and be in school? Can he drive? If he assaults someone (as he has done several times), should he be tried in juvenile court? Would he enter the record books as the first 6-year-old girl to have fathered seven children just as "Caitlyn" Jenner is now the first woman to have won the men's Olympic decathlon?

Equally absurd, but now equally necessary to respect, is a girl in England who on any given day may identify as a girl, Layla, or as a boy, Layton. She identifies as "bi-gendered." But she is not just a teenage prankster. "It isn't a case of me waking up and choosing to dress a certain way," she told the *Daily Mail*. "I've got no control over whether I'm going to be Layton or Layla on a certain day." And if you don't take her seriously, you're a beast and may be subject to prosecution. Such are the new politics of identity.

Part of the tragedy in such cases is that these people are cut off from the help they obviously need. Love has become, at the very least, morally unacceptable. The reigning ideology of self-creating autonomy cannot distinguish between living as you please and either mental illness or the effects of emotional trauma. For example, any clinical attempt to help youths in the turmoil of confused attractions understand their sexuality based on a religious or philosophic view of human health is condemned as "unethical" and "quackery."[34] In some states it's illegal.

This experiment will collapse under the weight of its counter-intuitive absurdity. Like communism, it is in such disharmony with God's order of creation that it just won't work. But also like communism, it won't fall without a staggering harvest of sorrow.

In the meantime, appeals to common sense will sound increasingly medieval. Modern Western culture has no intellectual foundation left from which it can call these behaviors insane. The church of Jesus Christ is the last bastion of sanity and the only hope of life for these wayward souls. But for it to be so, Christians must resist conformity to this world, renew their minds according to God's Word, and thus discern and adopt the mind of God in all things in the confidence of the risen and reigning Christ. And then suffer faithfully.

11. RELIGIOUS LIBERTY

The Fight for Religious Liberty
January 26, 2015

Many of those who govern us view religious liberty the same way they view gun rights: a holdover from the frontier republic and the buggy days of unenlightened barbarity. So they don't view these rights as "counting," especially when compared to more progressive rights that we have somehow discovered in the Constitution: the rights to abortion, same-sex marriage, and every means of sexual self-expression. They reduce gun rights to hunting privileges, and they tolerate religion only as a closeted ritual conducted by people whose opinions must, of course, be kept private.

But religious liberty is a hard-won freedom that has brought peace and civil decency to the Western world. We no longer have the oppression of religions and churches by an established religious entity, shaming itself and denying God's grace. Nor do we have states suppressing religion in favor of nationalism, drowsy consumerism, or vain moralism. But a legal and cultural war on religion will return us to strife and suffering.

Religious liberty is essential to the respect we show for one another as human beings. Thomas Hobbes believed religion is just the "fear of things invisible" that disappears with the advance of natural learning. Our ruling class today in government, education, and the media agrees with him. But there is what John Calvin called a *sensus divinitatis* that is part of our humanity, an innate awareness of God's ultimate reality, albeit often distorted and misdirected by sin. Alexis de Tocqueville called it the soul's "sublime instincts." He said, "Man may hinder and distort them, but he cannot destroy them." Suppress the stable forms of these instincts and they will emerge in radicalized, destructive ones. Our great French interpreter adds a warning. "The soul has needs which must be satisfied. Whatever pains are taken to distract it from itself, it soon grows bored, restless, and anxious amid the pleasures of the senses."

Members of the anti-Christian establishment (yes, Christianity angers and offends them; other religions do not) are not trying to replace a Christian America with a stolidly secular one focused on commerce and the bourgeois virtues that support it—thrift, honesty, and disciplined hard work. Instead, they celebrate the opposite, reaching hopelessly for the divine through ever more bizarre sexual license and other forms of novelty and unrestraint.

President Obama has made himself the national advocate for this new civil religion. In his 2015 State of the Union address, he boasted of defending not only political dissidents and religious minorities but also "people who are lesbian, gay, bisexual, or transgender." In the name of this publicly approved spirituality, the government has opposed Christian pleas to be spared having to provide abortifacients for their employees. Hobby Lobby won its case before the Supreme Court. The Little Sisters of the Poor are still in litigation. The Colorado Civil Rights Commission forced a Christian baker to provide business services celebrating homosexual weddings contrary to what he explained were his religious scruples.

Whether someone believes in the true God, no god, or 10 gods, he is no patriot who does not treasure religious liberty. Making this case will be the great battle of the 21st century.

Our Crumbling Religious Liberty

Monday, May 4, 2015

The alarm over our crumbling religious liberty in America, the land of liberty, is growing painfully loud.

We began awakening to how dangerous the world was becoming for people of Christian moral convictions when Mozilla executive Brendan Eich resigned under pressure over the discovery that he had quietly donated to California's Proposition 8 campaign, which would preserve that state's definition of marriage as being between one man and one woman. Phil Robertson survived a push by gay groups to remove him from the *Duck Dynasty* cast after he expressed his biblically informed view on homosexuality, but real estate developers David and Jason Benham found themselves without a television deal because of their religious views. Then came the wedding cake wars: A baker in Oregon faces a possible fine of $135,000 for declining to be involved in a lesbian wedding. When Indiana tried to pass a law protecting business owners of Christian conscience against such coercion, the activist outcry quickly neutered the attempt.

It's true that religious liberty has always been limited by what is consistent with civil society. In *Reynolds v. United States* (1878), the Supreme Court refused to accept the Mormon practice of bigamy as qualifying for protection under the First Amendment's "free exercise" clause. In *Employment Division v. Smith* (1990), the court denied that the sacramental use of peyote, a powerful hallucinogen, is an excuse for violating Oregon's drug laws. The state can also compel behavior that violates a religious conscience—e.g., military service and payment of taxes. But American society—at least the part that controls the economic, cultural, and political heights—is coming to view sexual liberty, especially liberties associated with the public acceptance of homosexuality, as redefining the limits of religious liberty.

Public opinion is shifting dramatically toward viewing homosexual relations, including within marriage, as natural, healthy, and thus socially acceptable. *New York Times* columnist Frank Bruni expressed[35] what many seem to believe: There is no war on Christianity, with many Christian denominations now accepting homosexuality as within God's will. Historically, he believes that what is within the bounds of Christian morality has changed or "evolved" with the progress of civilization, so it is time for the reactionary churches to fall in line on this issue and either "take homosexuality off the sin list" or be forced to do so. Bruni draws on the liberal view of Scripture, the progressive view of history, and the authority of liberal theologians like David Gushee. Why should secular Americans not see conservative evangelicals through this lens?

The Supreme Court will render its decision in late June on whether the 14th amendment guarantees same-sex couples the same right to marry that opposite-sex couples have (*Obergefell v. Hodges*). An Obama administration official admitted to Justice Samuel Alito that a decision in favor of this guarantee would call the tax-exempt status of Christian colleges, and thus their continued existence, into question. "It's certainly going to be an issue." They will leave us with only our churches … perhaps.[36]

In this time of cultural exile, Christians need a revised long-range plan: Trust our sovereign God calmly, preach the Scriptures faithfully, cultivate our families wisely, evangelize the lost consistently, and engage the culture winsomely.

Our Vaporous Religious Liberty

July 20, 2015

When the Supreme Court pulled a right to same-sex marriage out of the Constitutional hat in *Obergefell v. Hodges*, the justices also performed a disappearing act with the First Amendment's Free Exercise Clause.

In his 5-4 decision, Justice Anthony Kennedy reassures religious Americans their liberties are safe. They "may continue to advocate" against same-sex marriage. The First Amendment, he adds, guarantees "religious organizations and persons" may "teach the principles" of their faith pertaining to family structure.

We didn't need post-opinion commentary to see how these assurances are actually a death sentence for religious liberty outside the worship service. In his dissent, Chief Justice John Roberts puts believers on alert:

> The majority graciously suggests that religious believers may continue to "advocate" and "teach" their views of marriage. The First Amendment guarantees, however, the freedom to "exercise" religion. Ominously, that is not a word the majority uses. … Unfortunately, people of faith can take no comfort in the treatment they receive from the majority today.

Justice Clarence Thomas signals the same alarm. He may be providing grounds for a future court to blunt the illiberal force of the decision when he writes that the majority "indicates a misunderstanding of religious liberty in our nation's tradition." But they do no such thing. Thomas is dissenting from the learned and considered views of a Supreme Court majority, not grading an undergraduate Con Law paper.

It is not by a slip of the pen that Kennedy defended the advocacy of religious belief to the exclusion of its exercise. He wrote knowing the minority's concerns. So America may justly read his words as indicating that, yes, it is open season on anyone whose conduct reveals anything less than full advocacy of "marriage equality," regardless of religiously informed conscience in the matter.

Why was Kennedy's religious liberty passage even necessary given the First Amendment protections? Did he feel he needed to bolster them or was he signaling their coming contraction with a view to bolstering this great leap forward in social progress? The First Amendment shouldn't need defending, and yet now it does. For this reason, there's a bill before Congress called the First Amendment Defense Act … something like a castle of straw to defend against a dragon.

To make matters worse, in *Burwell v. King*, the Obamacare decision the previous day, Roberts wrote that words do not mean what they plainly say. "State" can mean a state or the federal government. Never mind what the law says. We all know what it should say. The First Amendment is also a written text. But if a text can mean whatever an imaginative justice wants it to mean, it has no meaning. And if words don't mean anything then, effectively, we have no Constitution.

Our liberties have come to depend on the generous feelings of a majority of nine philosopher kings and queens. But the church's defender is a greater King. The political right to live out our Christian beliefs in peace is a costly and precious heritage. At the very least, love of neighbor calls for a vigorous defense of that heritage. But Christians should prepare for more prayer, suffering, and choice between earthly and heavenly citizenships.

—Section III—

LOOKING BACK

1. BARACK HUSSEIN OBAMA,
44TH PRESIDENT OF THE UNITED STATES

The Selfie President
February 16, 2015

He's done it again. He stepped onto the stage and made a spectacle of himself, shocking the nation. No, I'm not talking about Kanye West at the Grammy Awards. It was President Obama, the man you would think knows better, given his unflattering words for the rap star.

The day after we had to evacuate the U.S. Embassy in Yemen, the White House released a playful video on BuzzFeed titled "Things Everybody Does but Doesn't Talk About." It features the president goofing in front of a mirror; using trendy expressions like "Yolo [you only live once], man"; and taking multiple selfies using a selfie stick. It was intended to grab the attention of young people and send them to HealthCare.gov to sign up for Obamacare before the Feb. 15 deadline. But the Yemen retreat was a national humiliation. Here was America, not al-Qaeda, on the run. Under orders from either the State Department or the Defense Department, U.S. Marines had to destroy their personal weapons and fly out by commercial airliner, presumably the reason they had to travel unarmed. It was also humiliating for the White House in particular, or should have been, because Obama had described Yemen as an example of his success in fighting international terror. The next day he seemed not to have a care in the world.

Not only were these images of the president fooling around poorly timed, given our disintegrating capacity under his leadership to address a collapsing world order, they seemed all the more dissonant when we discovered that he filmed the scenes the same day he learned that ISIS had killed Kayla Mueller, an American aid worker the terrorist group captured in Syria.

Obama has shown a pattern of insensitivity on these matters. It's as though he just doesn't care. He went before the nation to express his sadness and outrage over the beheading of American journalist James Foley ("Today the entire world is appalled"), only to split from the news conference straight for the golf course, where he continued his fun and games with friends. In this latest incident, the selfies say it all.

As we celebrate Presidents Day, we're reminded that the presidency is a serious calling, a high office with awesome power, entrusted to very few people. There is no higher honor or more demanding task than to govern a nation justly and faithfully. The U.S. president heads a sprawling bureaucracy that is difficult to monitor and manage even for the most attentive chief executive. The state of the world turns on his decisions and indecisions. The job is well paid and it comes with a nice house, a personal chef, and a fancy jet. But you are always on call and always in the public eye. It weathers the face and turns dark hair gray, but the ordeal lasts no more than eight years. It's a sprint, not a marathon.

The president does need down time, and golf really is relaxing. It's hard to coordinate golf and vacation time with unexpected world crises, but some days you have to cancel your round or cut your vacation short. And a light-hearted promotional video for an important and struggling program seems like a good idea, but not for the president, given his politically sensitive position and grave responsibilities.

But perhaps the president who is trying to appeal to self-absorbed young voters by behaving like one finds seeing himself in a cool video just irresistible.

Obama's Problem with Actual People

May 26, 2014

Barack Obama rose to office on a wave of messianic excitement that was unprecedented for Americans. It was as though this man, on the strength of his unimpeachable love for the people and for all that is good, would lift the U.S. government to the fullness of its promise and restore us to our collective humanity. And so when the ballots were in, we beheld the dawn and could finally be proud of our country.

Yes, in the minds of many it was like that. President Obama's wings have melted since then, and with his second midterm elections approaching he appears all too human and not at all the "god with us" his most ardent supporters had hoped he would be. In fact, he has been remarkably indifferent to actual people.

From the outset, he brought before us the sufferings of millions who had no health insurance and he called us to harken to compassion's cries and pass the Affordable Care Act. But when several million people lost their private health insurance because of the law and we ended up with about the same number of uncovered people, he showed no concern, as though the program, not the people, was the point.

In the Keystone pipeline delay, the president has sided

with the environmental activists against the bread-on-the-table concerns of working-class jobseekers and the tight budgets of everyone who drives a car or heats a home.

The Veterans Affairs hospital scandal is just the latest indication. VA hospitals, though required to see patients within two weeks of a request for treatment, were keeping applicants on secret off-the-record lists until an appointment could be arranged within the two-week window. In other words, to cover their bureaucratic tails they were falsifying waiting lists of suffering people. As a result, veterans who survived enemy fire abroad died of government neglect at home. The outrage has been bipartisan, with even liberal columnists like Dana Milbank throwing up their hands.

It was a month after the scandal broke and more than two weeks after the American Legion called for VA Secretary Eric Shinseki's resignation that the president spoke publicly on the matter. And then, despite Shinseki (now five years on the job) testifying before Congress that he is "mad as hell" over this and Obama's chief of staff telling us that the president is "madder than hell," the president delivered a May 21 public statement couched in conditional qualifiers that signaled he is unconvinced there is any wrongdoing in the VA system.

Nonetheless, he stated firmly, "Once we know the facts, I assure you if there is misconduct it will be punished." But that's what he said about the people who murdered our ambassador in Benghazi. As in that case, we have no reason to believe these assurances are anything but political deflections.

Obama's wing of the Democratic Party has never been keen on the U.S. military, but these vets are a cross section of the American people, drawn from every state, representing all ages and every race, Democrats and Republicans.

Perhaps from the start Obama has been all about Obama. He made his statement by rising to the presidency. He won the Nobel Peace Prize just for being himself and winning the White House. He did not refuse it. Having given us himself, he has given us everything. But he gave us Obamacare as well. Is it ungrateful of us also to ask for a vibrant economy and just treatment by our government as well?

The Obama Trust Deficit

October 20, 2014

With the midterm elections just weeks away, President Obama should reflect soberly on his approval ratings, just 40%, the lowest of his presidency, which indicate a trust deficit that will preclude any meaningful accomplishments in his closing two years in the White House.

He assured us during the Obamacare debate, "If you like your doctor, you can keep your doctor." Whether or not he knew this would not be true, a leader should not promise things he has reason to believe he can't deliver.

He assured us there was "not a smidgen" of corruption at the IRS, and this while a congressional investigation was underway. When we learned about curiously timed mass disappearances of sensitive emails from the hard drives of key players, fairly obvious signs of a cover-up, many wondered why the president was so glibly unconcerned.

The extraordinary amount of time he spends at fundraisers is unsettling, especially given the deluge of alarming developments at home and abroad. We understand the president's role in raising money for electing Democrats, and we are assured that the president is always on the job. Air Force One is a flying White House. Yet it's not the White

House and it's clear what his primary activity is on these frequent jaunts.

He plays a lot of golf. There's nothing wrong with a president relaxing on fairways and greens, but when he made a solemn announcement about ISIS after it beheaded two Americans and within five minutes was photographed laughing with buddies in a golf cart, what were people to conclude? Indifference to the matters he just addressed? He regretted the poor "optics" that he generated, but the public disquiet was over more than just how this quick transition to fun looked.

The general impression of incompetence hasn't helped him. The Obamacare rollout was inexcusably disastrous. It was weeks before he paid any attention to the VA hospital scandal. ISIS had swallowed half of Iraq before that threat from overseas made it onto his to-do list. Even the collapse of Secret Service effectiveness around him has been beyond his grasp. Perhaps he's just not that interested in most of what governing requires. He took us to war, then pursued it half-heartedly. When he talks to us at all, he speaks coldly to his teleprompter, not from the heart to the people under his care.

And now Ebola, a highly contagious and deadly virus from overseas. The president asks us to trust him and the institutions he leads, telling us, "I am absolutely confident that we can prevent a serious outbreak here in the United States." Some people will always trust him. Others never will. But much of the Great Middle has lost confidence in his confidence. So this begs the question: When he appoints a political operative as Ebola czar, making the Great Middle even more anxious, is he subordinating public safety to political calculations?

Leadership is largely about trust, but trust is fragile. Poor leadership destroys trust, and a serious trust deficit prevents any effective leadership. Until the president sees his popularity problem as a trust problem of his own making, the only progress he will make in the next two years will be in lowering his golf score.

Who Matters to the Government?

February 3, 2014

As healthcare savior, President Barack Obama is like someone who knocks a dozen people off a pier into the water in his careless rush to reach and attempt to save a group precariously perched at the end of it. He congratulates himself for saving some of them, but not all, while those he plunged into distress bob in the water wondering what just happened.

Obama makes a habit of publicly highlighting success stories for the major legislative accomplishment of his presidency, the Affordable Care Act. These people matter to him. This person had a preexisting condition, but now she's covered and she's doing fine. This fellow is covered because the law allows him to remain on his parents' policy until he is 26. The president told us in his 2014 State of the Union address, "More than 9 million Americans have signed up for private health insurance or Medicaid coverage" (a vastly inflated figure that CNN calls deceptively "squishy"). These folks had no coverage. Now they do. The success of these people is the measure of success. Obama called this "the real impact this law is having."

But 5 million people who were just minding their own business have lost their coverage as a direct result of the same law. They now have to seek new coverage through Obama's hopeless exchanges and entrust their personal data to a system that is transparent to every moderately persistent hacking identity thief. (Gallup has found that there are actually fewer people with health insurance now than there were in 2009 when Obama came to office.) But in the view of our government, these people don't matter. Tom Coburn, the GOP senator from Oklahoma and himself a physician, has been bumped by law into the federal health insurance exchange along with everyone else in Congress and has lost coverage for his oncologist. No matter. Millions of others have seen their premiums double or triple as a result of how Obamacare has affected the broader health insurance calculus. But they don't matter either.

When governments think their job is to equalize society—to bring about what they call "social justice"—it is ironic that some people always end up mattering more than others. As another great progressive leader once said, "One can't expect to make an omelet without breaking eggs." An activist government like this brings some down to lift others up. It not only picks winners, but also generates losers in the process. While this may be well intentioned, it inevitably becomes government in the service not of the people as a whole—the common good—but of particular politically supportive factions and constituencies. In other words, it becomes government in the service of itself and of those who share its interests. These governments don't really believe we are all equal at all.

Everyone should matter to the government of a free and equal people. When our government takes "equality" to mean everyone having the same liberty to exercise their faculties and employ their means, everyone matters equally.

Tyrants Among Us

April 16, 2010

What angers Americans in the Tea Party movement is tyranny. And well it should because it is spreading in Washington even more than usual.

Our Declaration of Independence still speaks for us where it says:

> But when a long train of abuses and usurpations, pursuing invariably the same object evinces a design to reduce them under absolute despotism, it is their right, it is their duty, to throw off such government, and to provide new guards for their future security.

Lawless government is an unmistakable sign of tyranny, i.e., government that exercises power not under law or according to the authority given to it by consent of the governed, but on an authority it claims to have in itself.

The recent healthcare reform legislation is an example of governing tyrannically. The law requires people to purchase health insurance if they do not already carry it, perhaps because they are young and healthy. This is not a tax. It is the government telling you to do something because they believe it is good for the country. It is not conditional upon any other behavior. It says, "You will do this or we will punish you with a fine."

I have not heard a credible argument from any elected officeholder justifying this provision constitutionally. Even the president, who has taught constitutional law, made only a vague reference to the state requirement that people buy car insurance. But that mandate is conditional upon owning a car for use on public roads. If people take the bus or walk, they can decline the purchase. But this is government exercising authority beyond what the Constitution allows, authority the people did not entrust to it. This is power exercised tyrannically, and on a grand scale.

At a constituent meeting, Rep. Phil Hare, a Democratic congressman from Illinois, stated with unguarded candor (as though it were no big deal) his disregard for the constitutional limits of congressional power when it comes to providing for what he thinks is the public good.

When asked to locate in the Constitution where Congress gets the authority to require everyone to buy health insurance, his response was, "I don't worry about the Constitution on this. . . . I care more about the people dying every day who don't have healthcare." In a half-hearted attempt to find a constitutional hook on which to hang the law after the fact, he cited the rights to life, liberty, and the pursuit of happiness, thinking that he was quoting the Constitution. When someone pointed out that these words are found in the Declaration of Independence, he expressed indifference to the distinction. "Doesn't matter to me. Either one."

In other words, when it comes to doing good, constitutional restraints are irrelevant. They don't apply. The legal constraints of the Constitution—in the eyes of congressmen like Phil Hare and, apparently, the president—are only for bad people. The goodness of the obviously good things that good-hearted people do with government power is the ultimate foundation of public authority, transcending even the Constitution. Another way of stating this view is that moral progress is the fundamental law of the land. It is the unwritten constitution behind the written Constitution. That is to say, the politically progressive use of power is self-authorizing. Every other exercise of civil authority must be subject to constitutional limitations because that is what a constitution is for.

This lawlessly self-flattering attitude seems to draw, but unfaithfully, from Cicero's maxim, *Salus populi suprema lex esto*, "the welfare of the people is the highest law." By *salus*, he meant the well-being or safety of the people. He was saying that because the individual depends on the community for the enjoyment of his private goods, and even for his very life, his individual good must yield to the public good in general when the two come into conflict. No law needs to state this. It is in the nature of the political relationship. In that sense it is the supreme law that transcends even the most fundamental written laws.

Cicero's maxim is one for emergencies, however. Both ends of Pennsylvania Avenue these days are governing as though it were the ordinary basis for legislative activity, or, to speak more cautiously, as though the fullest and immediate expansion of the welfare state were a matter of national emergency.

But in the face of such tyrannical usurpation of authority, such an obvious design to reduce us under the absolute despotism of benevolent technocracy does not justify violence. It does, however, justify vigilance. Every patriot should exercise that vigilance at the ballot box in November, asking him or herself the question, "Does this candidate govern or promise to govern under the laws, or regardless of the laws as a law himself?" Will this candidate govern as a benevolent despot, or as a public servant under law?

Let me hasten to add in conclusion that Christians are substantially to blame for this state of affairs. The constitution for the Kingdom of God is the Bible. In the late 19th century, Christians started debunking and dismissing its authority, and substituting enlightened progressive morality and the latest developments of scientific thinking in its place. Today, even Protestant Evangelicals, who supposedly have a high view of Scripture, treat the details of its teachings with careless disregard, following instead all too often the fashions of Evangelical subculture.

Christians can be salt and light by conforming their convictions more conscientiously to God's Word, and then voting their convictions more faithfully on election days.

The Imperial Obama Presidency
November 18, 2013

What if someone declared a war on check and balances, and only one side showed up? Apparently we would call it the Obama presidency. President Barack Obama's attempt to "fix" the health insurance cancellation crisis by telling insurers he would not prosecute them for breaking the part of the Affordable Care Act (ACA) that precipitated it is just the latest unopposed annexation of power by this most imperial of presidents.[37]

In February, under instructions from the president, Attorney General Eric Holder announced the government would no longer defend in court or enforce the 1996 Defense of Marriage Act (DOMA). Holder's letter to House Speaker John Boehner reads like a court decision. Obama essentially struck down the law, declaring it a violation of the Constitution's Equal Protection clause. In effect, he asserted a veto power the Constitution does not give him. He also exercised powers that belong to the judicial branch, namely the power to rule on the constitutionality of a law and declare it null and void. But constitutionally, the executive branch is simply to "take Care that the Laws be faithfully executed" (Article 2, Section 3).

He showed the same constitutional disregard in how he addressed the employer mandate delay.[38] The ACA requires employers over a certain size to provide their employees with affordable health insurance. When it became clear that the statutory deadline was hopeless to enforce, instead of going to Congress for a legislative fix, Obama simply chose not to enforce that part of the law. He exercised a power the Constitution does not grant him, though presidents have long asked for it: a line item veto. Asked if this was legal for him to do, the president responded, "Where Congress is unwilling to act, I will take whatever administrative steps that I can in order to do right by the American people." In other words, no.

In this latest "fix" to the ACA, by allowing insurance companies to restore the canceled non-compliant policies, Obama is reversing a rule that his Health and Human Services secretary added to the law after Congress passed it. This rule was designed to drive people with individual policies into the exchanges (precisely the opposite of the president's pledge). This was not an administrative provision to help properly execute the law as written. It is obvious from the disastrous consequences that it changed the substance of the law.

Now, on top of that, Obama pre-empted an impending legislative remedy with his own notice to insurance companies that he would not prosecute them for restoring policies. But he added conditions to that assurance, essentially writing his own law. In both these cases, the president has assumed legislative powers for the exec-utive branch.

In *The Federalist Papers* No. 47, James Madison wrote, "The accumulation of all powers, legislative, executive, and judiciary, in the same hands ... may justly be pronounced the very definition of tyranny." But, frankly, one would think that such an imperial president would have more to show for his efforts.

The Art of the Obama Deal: Just Do It

November 17, 2014

The newspapers reporting Republican victories in the midterm elections had not even been bundled yet for the trash when President Obama threw down the gauntlet on immigration reform.

We have almost 12 million illegal aliens in the country, about 60 percent of them from Mexico. Some have been living and working here for many years. Some, by childbirth, are now the illegally residing parents of American citizens. Some came here as children with their parents, and so find themselves illegally in the only country they have ever known. Some are criminals, perhaps in gangs, and some, no doubt, are national security threats. Congress has demonstrated by many years of inaction that it hasn't the capacity to address this matter that demands resolution for reasons of Christian charity and human decency, if nothing else.

These are fair concerns about a situation that has continued through several presidencies. Arguably, Obama had his first two years in office to address this issue when his party controlled both houses of Congress. Yes, he was working on health insurance reform and reviving the economy, but the relevant departments and committees were free to work on the matter.

The question is equally fair as to why he raised this issue immediately after the midterm elections and in such a confrontational manner. Why not challenge the new Congress to work on it over the spring? Instead, according to CNN, Obama has announced he will issue executive orders "to allow parents of children who are American citizens to obtain documents that allows them to stay in the United States legally, protect illegal immigrants who came to the United States as children and make clear deportation should still be the policy for convicted criminals." These documents and protections would involve work permits, commonly known as "green cards."

But the president has promised that "the minute [Congress passes] a bill that I can sign that fixes our immigration system, then any executive actions I take are replaced." But one suspects that "a bill that I can sign" means one that merely codifies his executive orders. Otherwise there would be great disruption and policy confusion from issuing and then withdrawing permits.

Obama's provocative announcement has left Republican congressional leaders understandably upset. They are concerned over the constitutionality of what Obama has signaled he will do. An executive order is the president's power to direct his administration in how to execute the laws. But he cannot order his agents to do anything not authorized by law, nor can he choose not to enforce a law. He serves the people by serving the laws to which they consent.

With millions of illegal aliens dispersed throughout the country, some prioritization of deportation efforts is required. But to affect by decree what was the subject of legislative controversy and to issue green cards under circumstances that the law does not specify goes beyond executive discretion to the lawless misuse of public power.

This American Monarchy

May 16, 2016

Voters are furious at how ineffectual and self-serving their government has become. Politicians campaign one way but govern another. They campaign for smaller government but it gets bigger with their support. They promise financial restraint but spend like fools with a stolen credit card. They confirm Supreme Court nominees whom they know will ignore the Constitution. Congressional committees rage about abuses at the IRS and V. A. hospitals, despotic decrees from the Environmental Protection Agency, disregard for the law by the Attorney General, and complete fabrication of socially revolutionary principles by the Supreme Court, and yet no one is impeached.

Much voter anger is over the failure of the Republicans to check the Democrats and of the Republican led Congress to check the President. Checks and balances are essential to modern republican government, setting one branch of government against another to prevent anyone from threatening liberty by overstepping their legal limits. Equally vital to liberty, however, is federalism, the separation of sovereign power between state and national levels of government. But the Dear Colleague letter that Obama's Department of Education circulated to nation's school districts last week concerning transgender students extended rule by executive decree throughout our political system.

Ostensibly, the letter was merely to clarify for local schools precisely what the 1972 Title IX law prohibiting sex discrimination in education means for transgender students, those suffering from gender dysphoria. "When a school provides sex-segregated activities and facilities, transgender students must be allowed to participate in such activities and access such facilities consistent with their gender identity." So it applies to bathrooms, change rooms, sports teams, overnight trips, and so on. Who exactly is transgender depends on the self-perception of the student in question, not the student's parents or a medical professional. Uncooperative schools—including colleges and universities—will face lawsuits and denial federal funds.

Of course, Title IX, the law to which the people gave their consent through their elected representatives, makes no mention of transgendered anything. Yet with this directive, the current administration in Washington has decreed that gender is distinct from sex and that whether one is a boy/man, girl/woman, or something else entirely is simply a matter of personal affirmation, not a scientifically ascertainable biological fact.

This is a radical change in American life. But there was no attempt to persuade the people or secure their consent. It was never debated in Congress. A bureaucracy—not even a court!—just imposed on us that our girls will share change rooms with boys who think they are girls, and men are now free to enter women's restrooms.

People are in the mood for revolt. But government overspending is not the fundamental issue. It is liberty, government by consent through elected representatives, not faceless bureaucrats. If no one effectively opposes this—states, Congress, private citizens through the courts—then we no longer have a constitutional republic. We have a democratic dictatorship, a kind of elective monarchy. This is the question for those seeking our votes.

2. GOVERNMENT

Progressive Greatness Only Through Government
June 3, 2013

Presidents can be puzzling. They campaign high, but govern low … except sometimes. They tack one way, then another. But occasionally they let slip what they're really about. Arguably, Barack Obama did this in his commencement address at Ohio State University last month.

The president's theme was citizenship, and he spoke of it in morally exalted and traditional terms: "a recognition we are not a collection of strangers; we are bound to one another by a set of ideals and laws and commitments, and a deep devotion to this country that we love." He highlighted the neighborly acts of "courage and compassion" occasioned by hurricane devastations and the Boston bombing.

From citizenship as private charity and initiative, he then presented it "in its fullest sense ... at the national level" as self-government, but defining it as something the Founders, whom he honored for it, would not recognize: progressive liberalism.

Political self-government is people governing their common affairs largely but not exclusively through elected and publicly accountable representatives. Obama captures this sense when he refers to doing "big things and important things together that we could not possibly do alone." He mentions infrastructure and space exploration. But in the next breath he moves on to public schools and healthcare, as if schooling and doctor visits also necessarily required grand, national undertakings. Give us your poor, your aged, your children, heck, even your periodic medical checkups, and we'll take care of them so you can breathe free.

He completed his rhetorical maneuver, saying, "We, the people, chose to do these things together—because we know this country cannot accomplish great things if we pursue nothing greater than our own individual ambition." Here he reduced all private action to individual selfishness. Great endeavors come only through government.

The heart of progressivism is the scientific administration of people's lives by those who know better, i.e., not only how to achieve public goals but what those goals ought to be. Progressives like our current president see every attempt to keep the administrative state small and accountable, and to reserve decision-making as close to the people as possible, as trying to "gum up the works," as he put it.

So does Obama favor civic participation or passive enjoyment of government care? He says he deplores spectator citizenship, generously quoting his Republican predecessor: "America needs more than taxpayers, spectators, and occasional voters. America needs full-time citizens." Yet that is precisely what the progressive state produces, unless participation means activism for further expanding the progressive state.

So it seems that if the dreams of our president come true through the OSU graduating class, our heritage of self-government or, citizenship "in its fullest sense," will be a civic life governed by the likes of the Internal Revenue Service, the Environmental Protect Agency, the Department of Education, and Obamacare. Inspiring.

Big Government: Too Big to Function

May 20, 2013

The biggest push to expand government from any administration since the 1960s is alternately unraveling in scandal and flying out of the grip of its makers.

A $787 billion stimulus effort got diverted into projects designed for political, not economic, payoff and speculative green energy disasters like Solyndra and Fisker Automotive, or was simply lost in the spending frenzy. Its healthcare reform law was so big and complicated that then-House Speaker Nancy Pelosi told us we had to pass it first to find out what was in it. Now we find that the Internal Revenue

Service, that behemoth of arbitrary government power, has been intimidating and suppressing conservative speech.

In "IRS Follows Obama's Lead," Jonah Goldberg reports,

"Drew Ryun gave up trying to get IRS approval for a free market organization after 17 months of bureaucratic stonewalling. But when he applied for approval of an organization called 'Greenhouse Solutions' he got the go-ahead in three weeks."

This corruption goes far beyond a small cell of over-politicized, low-level bureaucrats in Cincinnati. Anne Hendershott, a conservative Roman Catholic academic, was dragged into a Connecticut office for interrogation over business expenses related to her occasional pro-life editorials. The scope of this politically chilling campaign from the most terrifying arm of the federal government is nationwide. Meanwhile, the official who administered the offending division of the IRS now runs the IRS office that will enforce collection for Obamacare.

President Barack Obama claims he knew nothing of this until he saw it in the news. So is it any surprise that more Americans are suspecting that big government leads inevitably to rogue administration on a massive scale? Former White House adviser David Axelrod seemed to admit as much, saying, "Part of being president is there's so much underneath you because the government is so vast."

Government's job is to punish evil and praise good (1 Peter 2:14)—preventing nuclear attacks, enforcing laws for our safety against very bad people, and collecting taxes from people who don't want to pay them—so it requires a concentration of power.

But the power to protect is the power to oppress. Government of men over men is unavoidably human—all too human. People in government cover the spectrum of virtue and vice, excellence and incompetence, so to be safe they need accountability—the rule of law, democratic election, checks and balances, etc.

But safe government also requires proportionality. The other side of "too big to fail" is "too big to function." How well could your local school serve fifth graders if it were the size of the University of Michigan? Government needs to be scaled appropriately to the people it serves.

Government is good within a limited sphere. Proportionality means that government should not take on more than it can naturally handle. You don't give it tasks best suited for families or for God. With the national debt approaching a suffocating $17 trillion and the IRS thrashing out of control, the time seems ripe to consider the logistical limits to what we can do for each other through government.

Dysfunctional Government Starts At The Top

October 7, 2013

Leading Congress is like herding cats. As we move from gridlock to impasse to legislative roadblock in Washington, we're all wondering if yellow dogs wouldn't better serve us than our current field of public servants. What is it about our times that government has ceased to work?

Congress is an institution of 535 people who represent 435 districts and 100 statewide constituencies. Most of these people are up for reelection in 2014. Two-thirds of the Senate is not. And speaking of senators, most of them see a future president of the United States in the mirror each morning, and some very noisy ones are preparing the political soil for a 2016 run.

And that's the way it's *designed* to work.

There is no provision in the Constitution for political parties, but they certainly help organize the stew of popular passions, opinions, and interests, and the political ambitions that boil at the east end of Pennsylvania Ave. "Stew" is a deceptively appetizing word to describe our legislative branch of government. But our elected representatives reflect us, the people who elected them. And that suited rabble is what self-government looks like in an economically, philosophically, morally, and spiritually diverse and divided nation.

But there's hope for concerted government action, for movement toward consensus on the common good and the next step for the nation, and the Constitution provides for it.

The presidency is a unifying office—a single person, a single decision-maker with a single public voice and public face representing the entire nation. He has a special role in bringing Congress to consensus on major legislation through negotiation, personal relationships, and rhetorical appeals to those who elected them. That is how Ronald Reagan got a Democratic House to pass his historic 1981 tax cut.

But this quality of executive leadership is something in which President Barack Obama had no experience before coming to office and in which he has shown no interest since his 2009 inauguration. He has been a silent stranger to most of his party in Congress, and it was 18 months before he ever picked up the phone to talk with Senate Republican Leader Mitch McConnell.

This is a president who began his presidency rebuffing a modest opposition suggestion, saying, "Elections have consequences, and at the end of the day, I won."

This is a president who organized a televised bipartisan forum with congressional leaders on healthcare reform, but in the end conceded nothing. Nothing.

This is a president whose defining legislative accomplishment has been the historic and transformative Affordable Care Act, aka "Obamacare," a law for which he did not manage to get a single Republican vote. Is it any wonder there is a partisan standoff over it now?

Last week, the president called congressional leaders together at the White House to address the current standoff over the conditions for continuing to fund the government, only to tell them that there would be no discussion.

In a system of separated powers, when legislators in the opposite party stake out a negotiating position and the president can see only putting a gun to his head and holding "the economy hostage," one has to wonder if he understands the Constitution he swore to uphold and the democratic principles it embodies.

The president confuses campaigning with governing. A dysfunctional Congress is always a failure of presidential leadership. Behold headless popular government.

Liberty in the Crosshairs

May 27, 2013

The Obama administration is suddenly sunk in scandal. Not just one, but three. The Benghazi cover-up has been brewing since last September, but only recently has burst into the open with whistle-blower testimonies before Congress. But the Associated Press scandal, the Justice Department's widely cast seizure of journalist phone records, and the Internal Revenue Service scandal, the IRS harassment of conservative groups leading up to the last two elections, both came quickly on the tail of those testimonies.

It is quite common for scandals to emerge in a president's second term. National government in America is a sprawling enterprise and it is easy for some enclave of power to slip beyond the president's reach and go rogue at the public's expense. Or a president can fall under the temptation to stretch barriers and perhaps break a few. Scandal can involve a personal or financial indiscretion (Clinton's Lewinsky and Whitewater scandals) and sometimes political overstepping (Nixon's Watergate and Reagan's Iran-Contra).

But what distinguishes these last two Obama scandals is their attack on our fundamental liberties and thus on our form of government itself. Both involve suppression of free speech. (The press is a form of speech.) The IRS, by delaying applications by Tea Party groups for tax-exempt status, burdened the ability of these groups to make their case in the public square. Intrusive personal and political interrogations, and at times personal tax audits, intimidated not only these advocates of lower government spending but also opponents of same-sex marriage or of Obama himself. Do you remember how armed SWAT teams raided Gibson Guitar factories in 2011 to confiscate materials their Democrat-supporting competitors were also using?

The right to freedom of speech is an oddly American political experiment. Canada is a quite free society, but when someone asked a high official with the Canadian Human Rights Commission, "What value do you give freedom of speech when you investigate?" he replied, "Freedom of speech is an American concept, so I don't give it any value." Though Britain is the birthplace of modern liberty, notice this line in a BBC report on the anti-Muslim backlash following the butchering of a British soldier in London: "Three men … have been arrested by Northumbria Police on suspicion of posting racist tweets."

If people's freedom to express political ideas and support a political party puts them in the crosshairs of a powerful government agency, or if people are afraid of talking to the press for fear of discovery by a partisan DOJ, then politically we have become a fundamentally different country. In a free republic, the government is afraid of the people, not the reverse.

President Obama himself said in his first inaugural address, "America has carried on not simply because of the skill or vision of those in high office, but because 'We the People' have remained faithful to the ideals of our forbearers, and true to our founding documents." This is a crisis point in the Obama presidency. Will he lead us in a vigorous defense of those ideals and documents or become the founder of a decisively less exceptional country?

Bad Dog Government

June 24, 2013

Government seems out of control. That's dangerous for liberty. Government is like a good guard dog, a great asset when it's in your service, not at your throat; when it's on your leash, not on your chest. Effective but safe government requires somehow keeping the power to protect the people in the service of the people.

The issue in the Tea Party election wins of 2010 was out-of-control government spending, which is just the public tab for out-of-control government activity. With the national debt now almost $17 trillion [$13 trillion in 2010; over $19 trillion in 2016], this is clearly still a problem.

In President Barack Obama's second term, our federal government appears to be out of control on several fronts.

First came the out-of-control lavish spending on fun for government employees at the Internal Revenue Service and the Government Services Administration, the federal government's real estate and supply agency. The hardworking IRS spent $50 million on conferences over the last three years, including a $4 million training frolic in 2010. The GSA Las Vegas getaway now seems modest at just $823,000.

Government secrecy has become equally wild. High officials like Lisa Jackson, former head of the Environmental Protection Agency, used the name Richard Windsor to communicate covertly via a fake email account, apparently not an isolated practice.[39] This pseudonymous communication shields officials from public scrutiny and the Freedom of Information Act, and can hide their identities even from the people they are addressing.

Government surveillance of law-abiding citizens also seems out of control. The National Security Agency is keeping a record of everyone's phone calls, and a clandestine program called PRISM allows it access to our emails and internet use. The Department of Justice secretly snooped into journalists' phone records and charged Fox News reporter James Rosen with criminal conspiracy simply to get legal access to his phone records in connection with tracking down a national security leak.

Government bullying is out of control. Last year an EPA regional administrator was caught on video likening his "philosophy of enforcement" to Roman methods of conquest:

> They'd go into a little Turkish town somewhere, they'd
> find the first five guys they saw and they'd crucify them.
> And then you know that town was really easy to manage
> for the next few years. And so you make examples out of
> people who are in this case not compliant with the law.

The administrative state is one of the gravest threats to our liberty. *The Federalist Papers* No. 48 cautions that "power is of an encroaching nature." These fearsome federal TLAs (three-letter acronyms) like the IRS, NSA, and EPA have an unusual capacity for arbitrary action.

We need to update the Founders' project of limited government to encompass this "fourth branch," the sprawling modern administration. This time of multiple scandals may be our best chance to do it.

3. America and the World

Taking Russia Seriously
March 24, 2014

In the Ukrainian Crisis, Russian President Vladimir Putin is playing chess while President Barack Obama is playing peekaboo. Obama emerged from presidential fun like March Madness predictions and comic television appearances promoting youth interest in Obamacare to issue farcical sanctions against a handful of Russian plutocrats. The Russian stock market actually went up the next day. Essentially, Obama threated Putin that if he does not stand down, we will kick his dog.

Obama sent his vice president, Joe Biden, a notorious clown, to Eastern Europe to calm and reassure those virtually defenseless nations against the prowling Russian bear. True to form, the clown upstaged the emissary, and Putin had another good day.

Putin is looking for a military response from Ukraine so he can invade the country. He did the same in the Republic of Georgia in 2008. In Crimea, he is using Russian troops disguised as Crimean defense forces to seize Ukrainian military bases in Crimea and a gas plant on the Ukrainian side of the Crimean border. Putin is allowing Ukraine's 25,000 troops stationed in Crimea to make their way home but without their weapons—no guns, tanks … nothing. This was designed to humiliate and provoke.

Meanwhile, we refused a Ukrainian request for defensive weapon aid. The Obama administration instead offered military rations, meals ready to eat. He could not have sent Putin a clearer signal of either abject weakness or overt permission. Either way, Obama threw open the door and said, "Take it; it's yours." What is more puzzling: the lost Malaysian jet or what President Obama is thinking in this crisis? One is tempted to wonder whose side he is on?

Obama appears to be addressing the wrong questions. He has asked himself: How can we show international disapproval for what Russia is doing, thus to shame them into a return to good behavior. So he "stands with" the European leaders in "standing with" the Ukrainians. And in standing with everyone in this way, he reminds Putin of what good behavior means in these enlightened, post-historical times. We saw this in the supposedly tougher stance of his White House Ukraine speech, with statements like, "Russia must know that further escalation will only isolate it further from the international community" and, "Nations do not simply redraw borders … simply because they are larger or more powerful," and, "We want the Ukrainian people to determine their own destiny. …" Touching, one would think.

But Putin does not care about moral isolation, diplomatic frowning, and the principles of self-determination that his American friend has so helpfully reiterated for him. He cares about restoring Moscow's pre-1991 dominance in Eastern Europe, the Caucasus, and Central Asia. Putin has Ukraine by the foot, and he will bite and bite until he swallows the head. Then he will turn to Moldova and Estonia, a European Union and NATO alliance member.

The question for Obama is: What are you going to do to stop him? A rapid airlift of military hardware to Ukraine would be a good start.

The President's War

September 15, 2014

"I have the authority to address the threat from ISIL." So President Barack Obama affirmed in his address to the nation regarding our new military operation against jihadists who call themselves the Islamic State. But he also affirmed a few dubious claims like, "If you threaten America, you will find no safe haven." The jihadists in Libya are laughing as they sit by the pool over that one.

This is not just one of many drone strikes in a lawless region of a failed state in that vaguely defined 21st century operation called "The War on Terror." ISIS, or ISIL, is not a terrorist organization at all. It's a conquering army. Fighting it is "war" and requires a declaration of war from Congress.

The president has declared that he intends to "degrade and ultimately destroy" a distinct army led by a distinct leadership that exclusively controls a distinct region and calls itself "the Islamic State." It has a reasonable claim to being "a state," though certainly an unjust one established by unjust means. The fact that the Islamic State is, as Obama said, "recognized by no government, nor by the people it subjugates" doesn't change the fact. Destroying it will take the methods of war we would use to defeat any state.[40]

What the president proposes is not just a continuation of the Iraq war. Obama closed the book on that war and boasted about it. He brought our troops home and left no residual force. In his speech, he himself said, "This will not be like the wars in Afghanistan and Iraq." It's a war and it's not the Iraq war, and so the authority Congress granted for hostilities there has expired. Charles Blow at *The New York Times* called this "another foreign war," rejecting the president's evasive terminology, "counterterrorism campaign." He isn't even fooling his fans.[42]

To preserve the safety of government and the freedom of the people, the constitution requires a declaration of war. Under the law that governs every branch of our government and ensures our liberty as a self-governing people, the president may not use the nation's war-making powers in just any way he sees fit and against any people he chooses to identify as an enemy. The nation goes to war only after Congress formally debates the matter and passes a declaration of war.

We are heading into war without a vigorous public debate. Part of that debate might consider whether we have serious grounds for war. President George W. Bush had evidence that Saddam Hussein was concealing weapons of mass destruction and had the motive to use them. But Obama admitted that "we have not yet detected specific plotting against our homeland." What we do have are taunts and the intentionally provocative beheading of two of our citizens. We might also debate the wisest scope and objectives of the war.

In his Sept. 10 speech, the president illegally announced he is taking us to war. The fact that he will ask Congress to express what he calls its "buy in" to show the world we are united in the effort is simply a way of coloring this usurpation of power. The use of public power without legal authority, without public consent by the legally established process, is the definition of tyranny.

Obama's Terror Talk

March 9, 2015

President Obama has always been particular about the language he uses to describe jihadists. He renamed President Bush's "Global War on Terror" the "Overseas Contingency Operation." Granted, military officials objected to the old terminology because it magnified the threat of our adversaries and overstated their unity. But the new term was obviously designed to cloud what we were doing. This is the complaint against Obama's refusal to recognize the connection between Islam and most global terrorism today.[42]

At the beginning of his administration, Homeland Security Secretary Janet Napolitano was asked why she did not use the word "terrorism" in her testimony before Congress. She said she preferred "man-caused disasters" because "it demonstrates that we want to move away from the politics of fear toward a policy of being prepared for all risks that can occur." This was justly ridiculed.

The president himself has drawn ridicule for refusing to identify the religion behind the terror network that has occupied most of our national security attention since 2001. He refers to "violent extremism" instead of radical Islam. At his White House Summit on Countering Violent Extremism, Islam went entirely unmentioned. "No religion is responsible for terrorism," Obama forcefully declared.

In his essay "Politics and the English Language," George Orwell put us on guard against the intentionally deceptive use of political speech. Political leaders employ euphemisms and "sheer cloudy vagueness," as Orwell called it, to conceal what they are saying even as they say it, to indicate something while distracting from it. "The great enemy of clear language is insincerity," he wrote.

Obama caused outrage when he called the shooting at the kosher deli in Paris a "random" killing of "a bunch of folks," whereas the killer himself said he "targeted them because they were Jewish." When ISIS beheaded twenty-one Egyptian Coptic Christians in Libya, Obama lamented the killing of "Egyptian citizens," avoiding reference to the killers labeling the victims as "the people of the cross, followers of the hostile Egyptian church."

The religious element in the al-Qaeda conflict is admittedly awkward. It invites the appearance of being "at war with Islam" and tempts people at home to think ill of their Muslim neighbors or generalize about Muslims worldwide. Sensitivity to these matters prompted President Bush to rally the country to a "War on Terror" instead of to what it is: a war with Islamic jihadism. Charles Krauthammer mocked it, comparing it to America responding to Pearl Harbor with a "War on Sneak Attacks." Donald Rumsfeld himself, Bush's defense secretary, supported the term "global struggle against violent extremism." So the obfuscation has been bipartisan.

There is a time for the artful use of diplomatic language to address a delicate situation. But when an awkward truth becomes an elephant in the room, a wise leader addresses it squarely rather than continuing to veil it in the vain hope of persuading people to deny the evidence of their own eyes, and in so doing undermining his broader capacity for leadership.

President Dangerfield and the Patsy Superpower

January 11, 2016[43]

> "I tell ya ... I don't get no respect."
> —*Comedian Rodney Dangerfield* (1921-2004)

Barack Obama is our President Dangerfield. In world politics, he gets no respect. But the derision is earned. And as a consequence, the world is falling apart, and the resulting evil is spreading to America like wildfire to a California suburb.

Convinced that his predecessor in office, George W. Bush, had brought disorder to the world and shame on our nation by making us an international object of hatred, Obama has sought from the start to earn the world's love and trust. He began his presidency with an international apology tour. From there he followed a policy of "leading from behind." He looked the other way when the Green Revolution in the streets of Tehran had the chance of toppling the Mullahs in Iran. When Syria's President Basher al-Assad was bombing his own people into submission, our Commander-in-Chief drew a "red line" at the use of chemical weapons. But when evidence of this emerged and the Russians temporarily distracted from it with an offer to settle the matter, we walked away as though the subject had never come up.

In all this, Obama succeeded only in earning the contempt of rogues and tyrants who have stepped forward to fill the void.

Despite former Secretary of State Hillary Clinton's reset button with Russia and Obama's assurance to the Russian leadership of his second term flexibility, President Vladimir Putin has pressed his advantage in Ukraine and the Baltic states, challenging NATO's resolve.

Despite concessions to Iran that include a pathway to nuclear armament and the return of $150 billion in frozen assets with no deductions, the Islamic Republic seized ten of our sailors who drifted into Iranian waters on a disabled boat. Iran released the sailors the next day, but only after humiliating them—and their country—on their knees at gunpoint and later in apologetic remorse. This came after they fired missiles provocatively close to one of our warships in the Straits of Hormuz, which was especially brazen since it was just before the implementation of the nuclear deal.

China has hacked sensitive information from American corporations and millions of employees and contractors at the U.S. government's Office of Personnel Management without consequences. One is reminded of the British policeman who pursued a thief, shouting, "Stop! Or I'll say 'stop' again!"

Now the latest. By a series of mysterious events, one of our Hellfire missiles somehow arrived in Cuba from an ally in Europe instead of at home in the United States. The Hellfire is a powerful air-to-surface missile that houses highly protected, multi-target, precision-strike technology. Cuba's interest in the acquisition is the fortune that nations like Russia, China, and North Korea would pay the cash-strapped, communist nation to obtain it.

But this all happened back in 2014. But despite Cuba's unwillingness to return the misdirected package, the Obama administration re-established diplomatic relations with them anyway. To our international rivals, this confirms us as a pushover nation—the patsy superpower.

In *The Prince*, the notorious 16th century classic on political strategy, Machiavelli wrote that a ruler should seek to be both loved and feared, but "it is much safer to be feared than loved, if one has to lack one of the two." The reason for this, Machiavelli explained, is that "men have less hesitation to offend one who makes himself loved than one who makes himself feared; for love is held by a chain of obligation, which, because men are wicked, is broken at every opportunity for their own utility, but fear is held by a dread of punishment that never forsakes you." This is bad counsel for one's personal life but simple prudence in international affairs that are ungoverned by any enforceable law. God gave the power of the sword to governments for good reason.

After the disastrously naïve Jimmy Carter years, Ronald Reagan pursued a foreign policy of "peace through strength." In November, the presidency will go to whoever can convincingly promise to earn the world's respect abroad— from friend and foe alike—and so secure peace at home through the prudent exercise of American strength.

—Section IV—

THE CANDIDATES

1. THE REPUBLICAN PARTY

The Trump Effect

December 14, 2015

American politics doesn't seem to be making any sense this year. A blustery billionaire is leading the pack for the Republican presidential nomination and widens his lead with every breathtaking transgression of rhetorical decorum.

But there are no uncaused events in God's world. Something has produced what we may call "the Trump effect." On the GOP side, there's broad dissatisfaction with government in general and with the current administration in particular. (Democrats want more of it all.) When people lose confidence in the political system, they turn to a convincing boaster who doesn't care much about the constitutional system but seems like he'll make the trains run on time and kick butt at the border and beyond.

We have witnessed a steady succession of scandalous incompetences. VA hospitals have let veterans die for administrative convenience.[44] The General Services Administration treated itself to lavishly expensive entertainments.[45] Health and Human Services spent a billion dollars on a failed Obamacare website.[46] But Donald Trump, the billionaire developer whom everyone knows from the TV show *The Apprentice*, says he will run the country like a business.

People sense that politicians primarily serve their financial backers. Former Secretary of State Hillary Clinton, only the grossest example, sold her services for extravagant speaker's fees and donations to the Clinton Foundation, even from foreign governments.[47] Trump makes no secret of his massive personal fortune to signal that he is his own man.

Our political leaders tiptoe around the Islamic aspect of the terror threat. President George W. Bush assured us that Islam is a "religion of peace" and spoke of a "War on Terror"—a war not on the enemy but on how our enemy attacked us. President Barack Obama took denial to a whole new level. Fighting al-Qaeda became the Overseas Contingency Operation, hiding the whole thing behind a cloud of lexical smoke. When Maj. Nidal Hasan killed thirteen at Food Hood in Texas while shouting "Allahu Akbar," the administration called it merely "workplace violence." It was days after the San Bernardino massacre before Obama publicly recognized it as an act of terror, conceding only after the FBI forced his hand.

Most people can see that the terror problem is overwhelmingly a problem with radical Islam. They are tired of political correctness taking precedence over national and domestic security. Trump, by contrast, prides himself on being frank to the point of appalling rudeness.

In political desperation, people turn to outsiders, someone who channels their anger and seems candid and unsoiled. But are they looking where they're leaping? When a boy at a rally in New Hampshire asked Trump what his life would be like when he's older if Trump were elected president, Trump responded only that "Your life will be much better than it would have been if I didn't become president. It's as simple as that." In saying that, he thought he was saying a lot. But he said nothing about law, liberty, security, prosperity, morality, or harmony. The crowd cheered its approval.

H. L. Mencken said, "Democracy is the theory that the common people know what they want and deserve to get it *good and hard*." If voters have not been jealous for their liberty in the rule of law, it should be no surprise that neither our present leaders nor our aspiring champions ignore it.

Taking Trump Voters Seriously
March 7, 2016

"Trump supporters are bigots and racists and seem to have gone crazy"—so they say. That may be true of some of them, but it cannot be true of all of them, and not even of most of them. When one-third of a major political party throws its support to a flame-throwing boor like Donald Trump, it is wise to hear them out and take them seriously. "Let every person be quick to hear, slow to speak, slow to show anger" (James 1:19). Something's going on, and political leaders need to listen sympathetically.

Election after election, these people have seen their jobs disappear, while those who pledged to defend their interests have taken care of the donor class ahead of them. Free trade was supposed to be good for America, but while the economy is working for someone, it's not working for the people who now live from paycheck to paycheck and for whom a major car repair is a body blow.

People have been quietly irate at our porous borders that allow people of who-knows-what intention into the country. People also see lost jobs and lost loved ones to violent criminals. We can't keep them out and we can't get rid of them once they're in.

Our current president seems more concerned about what international Islam thinks of us than what we think of our vulnerability to Islamic terrorism. Trump voters see a harmless 10-year-old girl traumatized by an extensive pat down at the airport while 95 percent of weapons pass unnoticed through screening, according to a Department of Homeland Security internal investigation. And when they complain, they're called beastly names, told to be quiet, and treated as though they are the real public enemies.

This is madness to them. No one's looking out for them, and someone's getting rich or powerful—or both—from advancing their own interests in these matters over the interests of the ordinary people they're supposed to have entered office to serve. Peggy Noonan calls this political, economic, and social elite "the protected class."[48] They have no contact with the rest of us, "the unprotected class," and thus no real sympathy. We have believed their promises for a long time but received only ballooning deficits, stagnating incomes, cultural bullying, and legally unregulated demographic displacement.

A lot of decent people are looking past what others abhor in Trump to his kick-butt readiness to defend them morally against charges of bigotry, economically against industrial globalists, and personally against whatever strolls into the country. You don't hire a hit man for his moral pedigree. Their hopes are, however, entirely misplaced in this man, as he is every bit a part of the protected governing class—in his case, the crony capitalist wing—and gives us no evidence he will use his independence from donors to serve us rather than his own fortune.

Donald Trump may not get the Republican nomination. He needs a majority of delegates, but almost all his primary wins have come with only 30 to 40 percent support, earning delegates proportionately. If the nominee is someone other than Trump, that standard-bearer can avoid a tragic split in the party only if he can understand and convincingly address the deep concerns of Trump's constituency. If one-third of the party is upset at something, we need to listen.

What Evangelicals Get Out of Donald Trump

January 25, 2016

The arena at Liberty University was packed on Martin Luther King Jr. Day with a large crowd. Attendance at convocation is required for students, but the response to that day's guest, the celebrated Donald Trump, was considerably more than polite. Jerry Falwell Jr., the university's president, introduced the leading contender for the Republican nomination for president with the highest praise: "In my opinion, Donald Trump lives a life of loving and helping others as Jesus taught in the great commandment."

This reception, and Trump's apparent high level of evangelical support, 42 percent according to a *New York Times/CBS News* poll, is one of the great puzzles of the presidential campaign. Nonetheless, Trump's candidacy gives insight into what a sizable portion of white evangelicalism wants politically in 2016.

Since Ronald Reagan assembled his conservative coalition in 1980, evangelicals have united behind a social agenda opposing the sexual revolution and its monstrous prerequisite, abortion. To preserve their Christian way of life, evangelicals have also supported a muscular stance abroad and small government at home to protect against communist or Islamist invasion and secularizing governmental intrusion.

But now they are leaning toward Trump, the legendary New York City real estate developer and self-promoter. This is odd given his three marriages (Mark 10:2-12), lifelong love of money (Hebrews 13:5), deep involvement in the gambling industry (1 Timothy 6:17), and a publicly foul mouth (Ephesians 5:4), to say nothing of his past positions on abortion and gay rights.

On one level, evangelicals are like everyone else in the Trump camp. "Make America Great Again" resonates because America has become an international pushover. But Trump's defiance of political correctness appeals to evangelicals specifically. They are tired of being shamed by secular morality while Christian morality is shamelessly scorned and publicly condemned. They are concerned again for their way of life. The war against Christian bakers and florists and anyone—no matter how gracious—who offends a homosexual or a Muslim has believers looking for a champion.

Political correctness intersects with illegal immigration and terror. Trump's call for a temporary ban on all Muslim immigration caused a scandal, but many evangelicals cheered under the weight of growing Muslim influence and cultural privilege.

Seeing this response, Trump has been boosting Christian civilization. He began his campaign celebrating the Bible in general without mentioning specifics. With similarly vague affirmations, he proclaimed at Liberty University, "If I'm president, you're going to see 'Merry Christmas' in department stores, believe me." He vows to "protect Christianity" in lands like Syria, where Christians are being slaughtered. Other candidates have had strong personal Christian faith, but Trump, whose faith is obviously nominal, talks about somehow restoring the normality of Christianity. He's not clear on what that is.

In his address at Iowa's Dordt College, Trump lamented that "Christianity is under siege." But despite being a sizable majority of the country, Christians "don't exert the power we should have." Despite his previously distant relationship with the Christian faith, Trump is promising Christians a return to power and cultural dominance through his presidential intercession.

Contrary to secularist fears, evangelicals have never wanted anything resembling theocracy, but only a broadly Christian culture reflected in mores, the media, and public policy. But if we look to a tough guy president to deliver this, we absurdly expect a Christian country without the re-conversion of our countrymen. We want by strength of office what comes only by the weakness of the cross.

2. The Democratic Party

Business Class Socialists

February 22, 2016

Winston Churchill is rumored to have said, "If a man is not a socialist by the time he is 20, he has no heart. If he is not a conservative by the time he is 40, he has no brain." If that is true, then it's understandable why Bernie Sanders, the Independent senator from Vermont and self-described democratic socialist, is doing so well among young people in the Democratic Party. He won the New Hampshire primary with 87% of the youth vote. In Nevada Saturday, he picked up 80% of the under-30 vote. But by the same measure, given that Sanders is now 74 years old, those same Sanderistas have trouble identifying the brains in the field of presidential candidates.

But more difficult to understand is Sanders' appeal to the business and entrepreneurial class. These people make their living at making money. Their material success depends on a prosperous population with comfortable levels of disposable income. They should favor pro-growth policies, and they are all smart enough and savvy enough to know generally what those are. People tend to know what's in their interest, and yet many of them support candidates like Sanders who advocate wealth-retarding, redistributionist policies.

For example, in the last quarter of 2015, Bernie Sanders raised more money than his rival, Hillary Clinton, among the largest Silicon Valley tech companies. These were not calculated donations by executives hoping to buy influence with perhaps the next president. Instead, they were largely smaller donations from ordinary-though-well-paid employees at Google, Apple, and Microsoft.

The rationale of one young software engineer quoted by *The Wall Street Journal* may shed light on their thinking: "I want things to be fair, and I feel the system, as it is, is not. I have done particularly well, and I have a lot of these advantages. If you don't have them, it's really hard to get ahead."

His social conscience is common among decent, educated, accomplished people. He feels the weight of his moral responsibility to consider the effect of his decisions and advantages on his neighbors, especially the poor. But it's not the modern, secular worldview that grounds these moral sentiments. Godless, evolutionary materialism—the cultural default among the non-religious—justifies only selfish climbing with a prudent mutual respect for equal rights. The impulse to neighbor-love comes from the influence of what remains of our Christian culture.

But instead of giving to the poor by personal sacrifice, as the Spirit of God moves His people to do, the kindly secularist invokes and empowers the modern state, a false god and a vain hope, to lift up the downtrodden by taking from those on top, whether they like it or not, and redistributing it downward. It assuages the conscience at minimal personal cost, but rather than strengthening human bonds, it frees us from them. It substitutes robbery for charity, resentment for unity, and self-satisfaction for self-sacrifice.

Augustine observed that Satan is God's ape. He mimics God, but only to divide and destroy and enslave. God's purposes for us knit people together in peace, but only when pursued in God's ways with God's love. To allow for that, however, government must guard the moral space for personal sacrifice in personal charity.

Hillary Clinton's Machiavellian Moment

March 16, 2015

Email is dangerous. One is tempted to write things that one would never say in person. And email is forever. Even a deleted email is still there somewhere. People can keep the emails you send and use your words against you later. Cardinal Richelieu, chief minister to Louis XIII of France, said, "Never write a letter and never destroy one." Bill Clinton reportedly has written only two emails in his life. Hillary Clinton has been busy destroying hers.

Hillary Clinton's refusal to use a State Department email address while serving as secretary of state was a brazen violation of the law and in that way a puzzling compromise of her political ambitions. She installed the home server for her private account immediately after her Senate confirmation in 2009. At the same time, regulations were already in effect requiring all government officials to use official government email addresses secured on government servers.

In her news conference last Tuesday, Clinton claimed it was a matter of the convenience of not having to carry two devices, one for her personal messages and one for State Department communication. But this made no sense. Presumably everyone faces this inconvenience, but the law is the law. Also, she told an interviewer two weeks before that she carries an iPhone and a BlackBerry. Apparently, multi-device living is not a problem for her. Upon leaving government service, she was required by law to sign a statement that she had turned all official communications over the government, but there is no evidence, or even claim, of her having signed this.

So why did she do it? Hillary Clinton watchers observe that she is intensely concerned about control, in this case who can later review her communications. This is the defining feature of a Machiavellian. The 16th century political theorist whose name is synonymous with the devil (Old Nick) observed that the successful prince leaves as little as possible to the winds of fortune.

The prince wants his people to love him and fear him. But if he must choose between these, he opts for their fear, because whereas people love you at their convenience, they fear you at your convenience. You control it. The prince trusts no one. All of life is warfare, ultimately the conquest of fortune or chance. He cannot rest until he controls everything. And so he never rests and is perpetually at war with everyone and everything. Of course, the most successfully vanquished do not even realize how subjugated they are. Thorough deception is the most complete conquest.

There is a growing bibliography on the Machiavellianism of the Clintons.[49] But if Hillary Clinton is a Machiavellian, she's a poor one. The most successful fraud is the one that goes undiscovered. The well-used lie doesn't need burying by subsequent lies, each one harder to conceal than the previous one. The most adept prince is constantly deceiving people but enjoys the highest reputation for honesty and public service. This is not Mrs. Clinton.

You can't defend against the accomplished Machiavellian because his selfishness is invisible. But voters are without excuse for not weeding out the clumsy and obvious ones.

—Section V—
FINAL REFLECTIONS

1. Our Future in the Parties

Post-Republican Christian Voting
May 9, 2016

Christians don't see things the way others do. When you understand things not only by what is seen but also by what is unseen but revealed by God as true, when you take into account what is spiritual and eternal, your assessments and calculations are different. This is true in politics.

Since the 2012 election, America has seen major setbacks for religious liberty, a matter of no small concern for Christians. Last summer, the Supreme Court gave same-sex marriage nationwide constitutional recognition. There was already broadening persecution of Christians who hold biblical convictions on marriage and sexuality. Bakers are targeted and ruined for declining to supply wedding cakes for gay nuptials. A decorated fire chief was terminated for his published thoughts on the biblical view of sexuality. Christian colleges are pressured to conform to the normalization of sexual confusion. They are even shamed and punished for exercising their legal and constitutional rights on this front.

The now common rhetorical device for disarming religious liberty is to affirm it while denying that it can include any practical moral objection to the cutting edge of the sexual revolution. As Human Rights Campaign spokesman Stephen Peters put it, "Religious liberty is a bedrock principle of our nation; however, faith should never be used as a guise for discrimination."

The Christian's freedom to live consistently as a Christian—to worship but also to speak, to do business, to educate—is more important than the economy, illegal immigration, and even national security. But this has not registered in any way with the presumptive Republican Party nominee for president or with GOP officeholders lining up behind him for this fall's general election. Though Donald Trump has spoken in support of persecuted Christians in the Middle East, we can expect him to exercise his business instincts in New York City—fashion by accommodating LGBT pressure groups here at home. This together with his multiple wives, avarice, coarseness, disregard for the rule of law, and complete indifference to the mind of God in everything has evangelicals asking what remains for them in the Republican Party.[50]

Evangelicals got on board with the Republican Party because in 1980 the Republican Party got on board with them: government limited to its God-given sphere, opposition to abortion and the sexual revolution, and protection of private property and market mechanisms for encouraging the productive use of God's bounty. At this point, however, evangelicals can paraphrase Ronald Reagan: We didn't leave the Republican Party; the party left us—not only the office holders and officials, the so-called establishment, but also our biblically indifferent GOP neighbors.

The political fundamental for a Christian is that, as the Apostle Paul wrote, "our citizenship is in heaven" (Philippians 3:20). For this reason we "seek first the kingdom of God" and pray to our King, "Your kingdom come" (Matthew 6:10, 33). The kingdom priority is freedom for God's people to proclaim and live the gospel (1 Timothy 2:2). Perhaps we're past due for feeling out of place in America's post-Christian two-party system.

A New Evangelical Political Alignment
May 23, 2016

This is an election year and voting is a moral responsibility. God provides government for his purposes, and in a republic like ours he uses ordinary voters to do this. So the humblest voter has the moral responsibility to "think God's thoughts after him" when casting a ballot. But this year the choice may be especially difficult, at least as most evangelicals see it. "The lesser of two evils," they say, but who would that be? Others object that the lesser evil is still evil, and so they will abstain. Most evangelicals feel politically homeless in 2016. Our faith is under constant and multi-directional assault and no one is standing up for us.

The Republican coalition made sense for us in 1980. Turn aside the advances of the New Left with its aggressive secularism and ideological embrace of the sexual revolution. Reassert the Judeo-Christian moral consensus. But the New Left is now in firm command of the political, economic, and cultural heights of society. And they are on the hunt for non-conformists. So the political strategies of 1980 will no longer do.

Steven Wedgeworth suggests a new third party to advocate a more thoughtful Christian view politics and society.[52] It's a good view that he describes, but there aren't that many thoughtful Christians and it would be fringe party with zero influence. Some defender. I think Christians—white and black evangelicals, Catholics, and Orthodox—need a broader coalition centered on a liberty agenda, a party with clout that will defend us as a matter of core principle.

Americans in general can still appreciate their interest in individual liberty against the encroachments of an insatiably controlling state. The chief interest of Christians in particular is religious liberty. This is not only the freedom of worship that president Obama ordinarily concedes, but also parental rights, including the freedom to discipline and educate one's children as one sees fit, and property rights, including the freedom to conduct commerce according to one's calling and conscience.

Perhaps a Liberty Party could start with a breakaway liberty caucus from the Congressional Republicans and build toward a presidential candidate in 2020. The Libertarian Party is too doctrinaire, the political wing of an entire philosophy of life that reduces everything to an inviolable individual choice. That's what led to the sexual revolution and the current madness. But libertarians could be enticed into the alliance because liberty would be the focus—life from conception to natural death, property, and enterprise.

In 1986, I saw that public education had become impossible because education requires agreement on what a properly formed, educated person is. That was long gone. Now, in the same way, I see that a morally substantive public life itself has become impossible. Like any shared human life, it requires a common understanding of what at least morally decent person is. But we can't even agree on what a human being is!

This pared down view of politics is far from ideal and certainly sub-Christian, but it appears to be our best option for political defense against merciless assaults of the pagan political fantasy that currently holds sway over our land.

2. Our Future in the Culture

Our Declining Christian Consensus
April 27, 2015

The world seems to be going to the dogs. But according to Harvard professor Michael Sandel, it's going to the market, which can be the same thing. The market is great for efficiently allocating scarce resources but not so great for deciding moral matters. His book on the moral limits of markets, *What Money Can't Buy* (Farrar, Strauss and Giroux, 2012), has been in print for a few years, but our view of what is properly marketable has only become more slippery. The controversy over same-sex marriage is challenging us to face this intersection of markets and morals, and we are not handling it well.

It's true that the more disagreements we can leave to private choice rather than legislative coercion, the safer, freer, and more peaceful our lives will be. But can all moral controversies be reduced to private market choices? Are there some subjects that must remain matters for community-wide moral settlement?

Prostitution, for example. Is it just a contractual matter between consenting adult consumers? Can't I do what I

Smart Example

Using extreme/trigger ex.

want with my own body? If I want to exchange sex for cash, why not? A growing number are content to see it that way.

Should I be able to sell my children on the open market? Of course, they are not my property. But my parental rights are, aren't they? If I can surrender my parental rights by putting my child up for adoption, why should I not be able to sell those rights?

I have a vote in the next election. If I don't often use my vote and if I don't care that much who gets my support, why should I not be able to sell that vote, whether to a fellow voter or a broker?

Once you have seriously asked these questions, you have already crossed a moral threshold. You have passed into another moral universe where everything can be bought and sold on the market and the value of everything is reducible to its market value. Nothing is priceless. When things have inherent value—your chastity, your honor, your parental or civic obligations—it is you who must submit to them, i.e., your judgment to their value. Your relationship to a thing must conform to what is appropriate for it.

But we have indeed passed that threshold. We feel guilt for "forcing our morals" on others, and so we make a market choice out of what we once viewed as what's necessary for one's capacity to function supportively as part of a moral community. And so people have shrunk from their community-wide judgments on issues like homosexuality and even same-sex marriage into a market-based, non-judgmental stance.

But both of these developments—commodifying ever more of life and privatizing almost every moral decision—are symptoms of the declining Christian moral consensus. The poet William Butler Yeats wrote, "Things fall apart; the centre cannot hold." With no substantive moral foundation to replace it, nothing remains but the market, the emptiness of personal autonomy. This is understandable for decidedly secular people, and they have to live with the consequences. But the 75% of the country that professes Christ needs to square with how their Lord, who will judge the nations, expects people to live together.

Christian Cultural Dominance Through Weakness
July 27, 2015

The political arena is an angry place, where people contend with each other, for themselves and for their friends, over competitive goods like wealth, power, and honor. It is interesting, however, that Christians, the people whose Lord frees them from worry over these things (what we shall eat and what we shall wear) seem just as angry in their politics. Christians in America have been witnessing the loss of our historic cultural dominance, and we're upset. But the political fury of the faithful is not in keeping with the faith we profess.

Signs of this declining influence have been with us for decades at least. In the 1980s, organizations like the Moral Majority and the American Family Association attempted to reverse the decline. But these efforts failed completely, as seen for example in last month's *Obergefell v. Hodges* Supreme Court decision on same-sex marriage. Every "Keep Christ in Christmas" car magnet is a sign of this de-Christianizing culture.

By "Christian cultural dominance," I do not mean a society in perfect conformity with the perfectly biblical faith. I mean only a people that assumes various things about what is above us, beneath us, and within us—God, heaven, hell, the eternal soul—and certain ethical norms, regardless of how often they are violated, and all this consciously understood as deriving from the Christian tradition. In a Christian culture, biblical motifs find natural expression in art and literature. Except in rare cases, when someone becomes religious, he starts going to church. It's assumed. Evangelism Explosion with its diagnostic questions makes sense only in a context of Christian cultural dominance.

And cultural dominance is not a bad thing. We evangelize in the hope of many coming to know Christ. As God blesses those efforts, a predominantly Christian culture will naturally develop.

But we have been fighting to regain that cultural dominance as though it developed through political struggle in the first place. But it didn't. It came by God's gracious work in Christian witness: turning hearts to Christ one-by-one.

Perhaps God is positioning his church to rediscover the day of small things (Zechariah 4:10). God chooses the weak things of this world to shame the strong (1 Corinthians 1:27) and to show his people that he is stronger in his weakness than man is in his strength (1 Corinthians 1:25). God triumphs over his enemies by the quiet working of his grace (1 Kings 19:12). God's word to Zerubbabel was the same: "Not by might nor by power, but by my Spirit" (Zechariah 4:6). There is greater power in the quiet working of God's grace than in all the thunders and earthquakes of electoral and media triumphs.

A gospel-infused culture and rulers who recognize the Lord as God and take their directions from His word (Psalm 2:10-12; Romans 13:1-6) are great blessings on the just and unjust alike. But the church of Christ must not put her hopes in them. Even in our cultural exile, we live trusting God will do great works through weakness and small things.

The Good Life as a Political Agenda

January 7, 2013

Evangelical political conservatives over the last 30 years have fallen into an oppositional crankiness. Abortion stops a beating heart! (It does.) Two men don't make a marriage! (They don't.) Keep Christ in Christmas! (Obviously.) But the problem with the culture war is that we haven't accomplished much, if anything.[52] And for our efforts, too many people see Christianity as political and cultural nay-saying.

But the life to which Christ has redeemed us is a good life. It's the life of incomparable joy and human flourishing, though also of trials and suffering. Biblical is better!

God made the world good, but it functions at its best for us only when we use it in particular ways. If you want to go beyond walking and running to flying, you have to observe and follow the created order as it pertains to aerodynamics. If you want to build not only with wood but also with strong, lightweight plastics, you have to figure out how God made oil to behave under different conditions.

But God has given the world not only a physical but also a moral nature that, to be enjoyed, must be obeyed. Morally, some behaviors "work" better than others with a view to the good life, both for oneself and for a community as such. Christians may be more culturally preservative and even transformative if we focus on presenting that good life rhetorically as well as actively.

This leads first of all to a renewed focus on the life of the church as a biblically faithful and distinctly Christian corporate life. This goes beyond personal morality to how we live as a holy community, as the body of Christ. If your only relationship with people in your church is on Sundays, that's one of the first problems you need to address.

How is a distinctly Christian family a joyful nest for happy marriage and sweet, maturing children? People should ask you, "How do you do it?" You should be able to answer, "I don't. Christ does it."

How is a Christianly run business a better place to work? It should be obvious to your receptionist that her cheer and your godly management are closely associated. Your workers should greet any call to unionization with puzzled stares.

How is it life-enhancing when the love of a Christian community addresses the needs of the needy? The early church took in orphans. Today's church can take in single mothers and wandering, fatherless young men. Christians can reduce government budget deficits by making government social action unnecessary.

There are believers and churches everywhere criss-crossing economic classes, theological traditions, and ethnic backgrounds. It should not be difficult to make the beauty and goodness of Christ obvious.

Like any father's watchful supervision of his children, God's commands are for our good. It's an American truism that if you build a better mousetrap, the world will beat a path to your door. The good life is a promising campaign.

3. Our Future as the Church

The Call for a "Benedict Option"

June 1, 2015

My teenage kids see homosexual couples getting married on the news. They hear about Christian businesses being vilified for wanting to do business Christianly. So I explained to them that they are living at a turning point in Western civilization, and it will not turn back. This is the new world—their world—and it is unfriendly to their faith.

So how then shall they live? Rod Dreher, an Eastern Orthodox conservative columnist has suggested the "Benedict Option."[53]

There has been a movement in the last 350 years of modern life toward ever-greater individual autonomy and thus the disintegration of Christian authority (Bible, tradition, church). This development is approaching its nadir before our eyes. Christians fought it in the modernist controversy 100 years ago. The Lord sent us Abraham Kuyper, G. K. Chesterton, and C. S. Lewis to name the problem and arm us against it. Jerry Falwell's Moral Majority fought the symptoms while often carrying the disease.

Now a new paganism, launched into its final stage of development by the sexual revolution, is redefining the nature of marriage and family, the foundation of society, so as to include homosexual unions and polygamy, and thus is changing how we view ourselves at the deepest level—what it means to be male and female or whether there even are such things. This builds on a previous Darwinian assault that convinced us to see ourselves as merely sophisticated beasts, and a Nietzschean assault that persuaded us that nothing is true and thus we are all free to create our own values and even ourselves.

Now slightly more than half of Americans believe that same-sex marriage is acceptable. But that figure conceals a significant groundswell: 80% of young people support it. Even in Louisiana, the most religious, church-attending state in the union, most people under the age of 35 believe that homosexual couples should be able to marry. University of Notre Dame sociologist Christian Smith says the reason is that most American teens (and they're not alone) are "moralistic therapeutic deists." Dreher summarizes the tenets of this popular substitute for Christianity: "God exists, and he wants us to be nice to each other, and to be happy and successful."[54]

In view of this, the culture warriors are exhausted and discouraged the way the defenders of Gondor were when the hammer-wielding trolls burst through the gates in *Lord of the Rings: The Return of the King.* So Dreher's call to the Benedict Option has appeal: The fight is lost; an apostate Christendom has chosen the darkness of its self-entranced imagination over the Prince of Life and the good world as He gave it to us. Let's treasure what is left and secure it for a better day. Let's cultivate our families and our churches, and develop a flourishing Christian sub-culture as a testimony to the world and a haven for the hungry.

The Argument for the "Benedict Option"

June 8, 2015

America has leapt quickly from feminist egalitarianism to same-sex marriage and now to teaching "gender fluidity" and "gender spectrum" as facts of life in the public schools. The advance of sexual nihilism against Christian culture and orthodoxy—its mortal foes—seems limited only by the boldness of the modern imagination.

In response, Rod Dreher suggests the "Benedict Option." Benedict was a sixth century young nobleman who withdrew to the wilderness from the iniquity of Rome, 25 years after the fall of the empire, in pursuit of a fuller Christian devotion. He established isolated communities—the first monasteries—that functioned as conservatories of faith, learning, and civilization. Arguably, in the long run, he saved the Western world.

Western civilization is again—but in a different way—hostile to the greatest treasures of heart, mind, and spirit. We have been aggressive at the polls and in the courts while neglecting the integrity of our families, the Christian education of our children, and their exposure to cultural toxins, and allowing our churches to become extensions of the service and entertainment industries. It is time for Christians, Dreher argues, to execute a strategic withdrawal—perhaps for generations—from attempting to recover our cultural dominance. He describes it as "a radical shift in perspective among Christians, one in which we see ourselves as living in the ruins (though very comfortable ones!) of Christian civilization, and tasked with preserving the living faith through the coming Dark Ages."[55]

He does not have in mind an Amish-like isolation, despite his praise for people who haul off to Alaska to be part of a tightly knit Eastern Orthodox parish.[56] Nor does he intend a neo-fundamentalist separation. It is not a "Bunker Option," any more than cultivating a thriving and hospitable Christian home is a bunkered domestic life.

The Benedict Option has three elements: re-centered Christian identity, attractive community witness, and defensive political engagement. Dreher calls it "a new and concentrated *inwardness* so that we can strengthen our communal lives and our *outward* witness and service to the broader culture."[57] His call is to rediscover what should have been our focus all along: the Christ-headed community that sustains us in our precious faith, matures our understanding of it, and enables our consistent practice of it. In this way, Dreher's Benedict Option is both preservative and proclamatory.

Politically, it entails "a strong recalibration on the part of Christians of what is possible through politics in a liberal order."[58] This recalibrated effort nonetheless calls for aggressive defense of religious liberty, e.g., through organizations like Alliance Defending Freedom. In the almost half-century of culture-warring, we left our rear flank exposed. Dreher is calling us to fortify that flank while maintaining a defensive stance on the political front, all while flinging wide open the doors of the city to receive refugees from the Dark Lord's territory.

Only when Christians more credibly understand themselves as the church and live more consistently in that will the crown rights of Christ become appealing to a spiritually destitute populace.

The "Benedict Option" or the "Jeremiah Mandate"?

June 15, 2015

Babylon is a town on Long Island in New York. What were these people thinking when they named their town after a dissolute, pagan, ancient Near Eastern imperial capital. But in light of recent cultural developments, it makes sense. Perhaps they were not celebrating sin but recognizing themselves as God's people sojourning in a modern Babylon. That is indeed where we are.

Rod Dreher at *The American Conservative* advocates the "Benedict Option" for dealing with this, a withdrawal from the culture wars to a re-deepening in the Christian life, personally and corporately, not only for our own sakes and for the sake of God's glory, but also so we have something substantial and holy to offer a misguided world.

A Christian turn inward is no guarantee the secular

revolutionaries will not chase us into our schools, colleges, ministries, and other institutions, even our families, where we preserve and cultivate our covenant communities. For this reason, Dreher stresses the need for a politically and legally defensive repositioning to protect these institutions.

It explains much of our present condition that we can speak of this proposal as a radical departure from ordinary Christian practice. Much of this is nothing other than a full-orbed, consistent Christian life. But most churchgoers are only faintly aware of this culture clash, this conflict of kingdoms, and what it should cost them in their discipleship.

But what does the defensive cultural and political stance of the Benedict Option look like in practice? I teach at The King's College, where our goal is to prepare students to help shape and perhaps lead strategic institutions. We have alumni at *National Review* and *The Blaze*, the Manhattan Institute, major publishing and investment firms, and Harvard and Yale law schools. If they can, why should they not? A bird must fly and a racehorse has to run. These are legitimate callings and great privileges. In these settings, grads will conduct themselves Christianly and bring the mind of Christ to bear on their governing responsibilities with, God willing, transformative effects.

Should we dissuade Christians from seeking elective office? If they succeed, should they not advocate godly policies as best they can? As voters, should we not make God's voice heard in the public square—His square, after all—as we have learned it in His Word? God gave His people a "Jeremiah Mandate" for their exile in Babylon, "Seek the welfare of the city where I have sent you into exile [in our case, internal cultural exile], and pray to the LORD on its behalf, for in its welfare you will find your welfare" (Jeremiah 29:7).

Dreher is right that we have entered a new phrase of Western history and there is no going back anytime soon. We should labor faithfully in our callings and labor in hope, "for it is God who works in you, both to will and to work for his good pleasure" (Philippians 2:13). But at this point, especially given the last 35 years, we can have no reasonable hope of "taking back America" for Christian culture. But there is always hope in the gospel itself and the cultural fruits that follow.

Following Jesus the Public Enemy

May 18, 2015

So here we are. Distinctly Christian morality has become socially unacceptable, and it is wise in some workplaces to keep one's Christian identity in the closet.

There are some whose thoughts will fly to the Lord's Second Coming. That is "our blessed hope" (Titus 2:13), but it is speculative to think it is near. People were sure of its imminence during the Black Death in the 14th century and during World War I and II. But it is possible that we are still in the early church.

So how then shall Christians conduct themselves in the 21st century? Accepting the new moral and cultural norms is the easy route, but it is apostasy: "… what partnership has righteousness with lawlessness? Or what fellowship has light with darkness? What accord has Christ with Belial? …" (2 Cor. 6:14-15).

Christians must take their holiness more seriously, their difference from the world around them, their life as sojourners (Ephesians 2:19), or they will go the way of the 20th century's respectable churches: from mainline to sideline to flatline. Taking ourselves seriously as children of light in a time of descending darkness involves seven commitments:

1. Trust our sovereign God calmly. Christ's church has persevered for 2,000 years through persecution, heresy, schism, worldliness, as well as Muslim invasions and modern rationalism because it is not a human movement but a divine work of God's Spirit. "Fear not, little flock," says our Lord, "for it is your Father's good pleasure to give you the kingdom" (Luke 12:32).

2. Preach the Scriptures faithfully. Carl Trueman writes, "Those who are deeply grounded in their Christian identity by their churches on a Sunday will think more clearly about how to respond to the challenges they face Monday to Saturday." Our Lord prayed for us: "Sanctify them in the truth. Your word is truth" (John 17:17).[59]

3. Cultivate our families wisely. Neither the public schools nor the neighbor child's parents—much less teen lit, the internet, or anything on TV—will support your efforts to disciple your children in Christ. Tell your children who they are and that they are different. Tell them, "These are your people," then demonstrate your commitment to your Christian community and conduct yourself in a way that testifies to their indwelling Lord and Savior.

4. Evangelize the lost consistently. Christ will build His church and the gates of hell will not prevail against it. Concede no ground. David did not cower with the others when pagan Goliath appeared dominant. He defied him and "ran quickly toward the battle line to meet the Philistine" (1 Samuel 17:48).

5. Engage the culture joyfully and boldly. It's easy to condemn drunkenness when everyone, even the drunks, knows that it's wrong. But it takes courage of conviction to call people out of the jealous embrace of their right to self-creation.

6. Suffer for Christ patiently. You cannot expect the fanatics of modernism to respond softly to your winsomeness.[60] They crucified our Lord, though He was perfectly lovable, because He denied their right to set their own course (Psalm 2:3) and make a name for themselves (Genesis 11:4).

7. Govern for Christ justly. Voting is an exercise of government, of serving God in his administration of order and justice. So seek to grow in civic wisdom. Vote knowledgably and strategically. Attend town council and school board meetings. Seek election to these bodies. Govern your country and community through prayer (Jeremiah 29:7).

Closing Comment

We seem to be living in a mad, mad, mad, mad world. But whereas in the 1963 film of that title the crew of clowns had the whispered clue of a dying man to guide them, Christians have the Word of God, entirely true and trustworthy. Buddy Hackett and friends had the hope of a buried fortune to encourage them through their wild adventure, but we have a more excellent treasure—Christ, the hope of glory.

Moreover, while the world may have lost its bearings, the universe remains in proper order under God's unruffled government. From age to age He builds his church without fail and works all things together for the good of his people. And the Apostle's good word to the struggling church in pagan Rome is also welcome in our day: "*May the God of hope fill you with all joy and peace in believing, so that by the power of the Holy Spirit you may abound in hope*" (Romans 15:13).

ENDNOTES

1. "The Europe Syndrome and the Challenge to American Exceptionalism," www.aei.org, March 16, 2009, adapted from his 2009 Irving Kristol Lecture delivered in Washington, D.C. on March 11, 2009.

2. Michael Barone, "America is Two Countries, Not on Speaking Terms," www.washingtonexaminer.com, November 6, 2012.

3. *After Virtue* (University of Notre Dame Press, 1981); p.252.

4. Franklin Delano Roosevelt, *State of the Union Address*, January 11, 1944.

5. George F. Will, "The Danger of a Government with Unlimited Power," *Washington Post*, June 3, 2010.

6. Harry McClintock, "In the Big Rock Candy Mountains" (1928).

7. "Break the Immigration Impasse," *Wall Street Journal*, July 10, 2014.

8. "Woman Caught on Video Unleashing Violent Tirade on Pro-Life Activists," www.theblaze.com, July 10, 2014.

9. *Beyond Red vs Blue: The Political Typology*, www.people-press.org, June 26, 2014.

10. D.C. Innes, "What I Saw at the Naturalization," *Washington Times*, March 16, 2010.

11. Peter Wood, *A Bee in the Mouth: Anger in America Today*, New York: Encounter Books, 2007.

12. "How to Understand Politics," *First Things*, August 2007.

13. Christopher Caldwell, *Reflections on the Revolution in Europe: Immigration, Islam, and the West* (Doubleday, 2009).

14. "The Crisis of World Order," *Wall Street Journal*, November 20, 2015.

15. "Trump's Incoherent, Inconsistent, Incomprehensible Foreign Policy," *Washington Post,* April 28, 2016.

16. D. C. Innes, "The Patsy Superpower," *The Daily Caller*, January 14, 2016.

17. "Why Putin Fears Ukraine: It's an Alternative Russia," *Wall Street Journal*, March 7, 2014.

18. "The Eurasianist Threat," *National Review*, March 3, 2014.

19. Neil Shah, "Baby Bust Threatens Growth," *Wall Street Journal,* December 4, 2014.

20. David Brooks, "The Republican Glasnost," *New York Times*, December 6, 2012.

21. Jonathan Last, "America's Baby Bust," *Wall Street Journal,* February 12, 2013.

22. Rich Lowry, "Books Without Borders," www.nationalreview.com, July 22, 2011.

23. Shane Harris, "What We Know About the NSA Metadata Program," www.washingtonian.com, June 6, 2013; Jonah Goldberg, "What is the NSA Doing with All This Surveillance?," *Newsday*, June 6, 2013.

24. Rick Lowry, "Climate Alarmism Acknowledges Doubt," *National Review*, February 16, 2010; Timothy Lamar, "Cooking Up a Heatwave," Worldmag.com, December 19, 2009.

25. Nicolas Loris, "Energy Production on Federal Lands," www.heritage.org, June 27, 2013.

26. Dave Andrews, "On the Immorality of Fracking," www.sojo.net, September 20, 2011.

27. "Green Energy Hurts the Poor," www.world.wng.org, July 2, 2013.

28. "Sons of Divorce, School Shooters," *National Review*, December 16, 2013.

29. John M. Perkins, *Let Justice Roll Down* (Regal Books, 1976).

30. D. C. Innes, "A Year of Racial Strife," www.world.wng.com, December 29, 2014.

31. George L. Kellering and James Q. Wilson, "Broken Windows: the Police and Neighborhood Safety," *The Atlantic* (March 1982); George L. Kellering and William J. Bratton, "Why We Need Broken Windows Policing," *City Journal* (Winter 2015).

32. "Another Tipping Point: Birth Outside Marriage," *The Aquila Report*, February 23, 2012.

33. Rod Dreher, "Transgender Babies: the New Civil Rights Frontier," *The American Conservative*, June 27, 2014.

34. Robert Carle, "When Government Keeps Teens for Seeking a Therapist," *The Public Discourse*, November 14, 2013.

35. "Bigotry, the Bible, and the Lessons of Indiana" (April 3, 2015).

36. Joe Carter, "How the Federal Government May Put Christian Schools Out of Business," www.blog.acton.org, April 29, 2015; "Sermons on Biblical Sexuality Illegal in Iowa?," www.ADFmedia.org, July 5, 2016.

37. I have taken this phrase from Arthur M. Schlesinger Jr's book on Richard Nixon, *The Imperial Presidency* (1973).

38. George F. Will, "Obama's Unconstitutional Steps Worse Than Nixon's," *Washington Post*, August 14, 2013.

39. Thomas Lifson, "Obama Administration May Have a Fourth Big Scandal," www.americanthinker.com, June 4, 2013.

40. Angelo Codevilla, "If You Want to Stop ISIS, Here Is What It Will Take," www.thefederalist.com, August 25, 2014.

41. Nicholas Kristof, "Critique from an Obama Fan," *New York Times*, September 10, 2014.

42. David Frum, "Why Obama Won't Talk About Islamic Terrorism," *The Atlantic*, February 16, 2015.

43. This essay combines the "President Dangerfield" column in Worldmag.com with my article, "The Patsy Superpower," in *The Daily Caller*, January 14, 2016.

44. Curt Devine, "307,000 Veterans May Have Died Awaiting Veterans Affairs Health Care, report says," www.cnn.com, September 3, 2015.

45. Lisa Rein and Joe Davidson, "GSA chief resigns amid reports of excessive spending," *Washington Post*, April 2, 2012.

46. Alex Wayne, "Obamacare Website Costs Exceed $2 Billion, Study Finds," www.bloomberg.com, September 24, 2014.

47. Rick Moran, "Before Seeking the Presidency, Hillary Ran a Pay for Play Scheme," www.americanthinker.com, May 17, 2015.

48. "Trump and the Rise of the Unprotected," *Wall Street Journal*, February 25, 2016.

49. For example, Michael Barone, "Bill, Meet Niccolo," *U.S. News and World Report*, September 10, 1995; Richard Reeves, "He's Machiavellian, and That's a Compliment," *Baltimore Sun*, May 28, 1997; Ron Rosenbaum, "So What if Hillary is Machiavellian, We Need 'Princess,'" *Observer*, November 13, 2006.

50. Matthew Lee Anderson, "Evangelicalism After Trump: the Moral Bankruptcy of the GOP," *Mere Orthodoxy*, May 4, 2016; Steven Wedgeworth, "Evangelicalism After Trump: Now is the time to escape from the GOP," *Mere Orthodoxy*, May 6, 2016.

51. "Evangelicalism After Trump: Now is the time to escape from the GOP," *Mere Orthodoxy*, May 6, 2016.

52. Cal Thomas and Ed Dobson, *Blinded By Might: Why the Religious Right Can't Save America* (Zondervan, 1999).

53. Summarized in Damon Linker, "The Benedict Option: Why the religious right is considering an all-out withdrawal from politics," www.theweek.com, May 19, 2015.

54. "Christian and Countercultural," *First Things* (February 2015).

55. Ibid.

56. "Benedict Option: a medieval model inspires Christian communities today," *The American Conservative*, December 12, 2013.

57. "The Benedict Option and Antipolitical Politics," *The American Conservative*, May 19, 2015.

58. Ibid.

59. "Protest and Survive, But How?," *First Things*, May 5, 2015.

60. Rod Dreher, "The Failure of Winsomeness," *The American Conservative*, May 6, 2015.

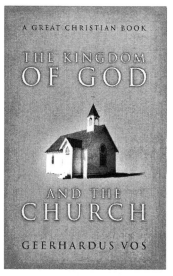

THE MISSION OF GREAT CHRISTIAN BOOKS

The ministry of Great Christian Books was established to glorify The Lord Jesus Christ and to be used by Him to expand and edify the kingdom of God while we occupy and anticipate Christ's glorious return. Great Christian Books will seek to accomplish this mission by publishing Gospel literature which is biblically faithful, relevant, and practically applicable to many of the serious spiritual needs of mankind upon the beginning of this new millennium. To do so we will always seek to boldly incorporate the truths of Scripture, especially those which were largely articulated as a body of theology during the Protestant Reformation of the sixteenth century and ensuing years. We gladly join our voice in the proclamations of— Scripture Alone, Faith Alone, Grace Alone, Christ Alone, and God's Glory Alone!

Our ministry seeks the blessing of our God as we seek His face to both confirm and support our labors for Him. Our prayers for this work can be summarized by two verses from the Book of Psalms:

"...let the beauty of the LORD our God be upon us, And establish the work of our hands for us; Yes, establish the work of our hands." —Psalm 90:17

"Not unto us, O LORD, not unto us, but to your name give glory. —Psalm 115:1

Great Christian Books appreciates the financial support of anyone who shares our burden and vision for publishing literature which combines sound Bible doctrine and practical exhortation in an age when too few so-called "Christian" publications do the same. We thank you in advance for any assistance you can give us in our labors to fulfill this important mission. May God bless you.

For a large selection of other
great Christian books—

contact us in
any of the following ways:

write us at:
Great Christian Books
160 37th Street
Lindenhurst, NY 11757

call us at:
(631) 956-0998

find us online:
www.greatchristianbooks.com

email us at:
mail@greatchristianbooks.com

39323799R00099

Made in the USA
Middletown, DE
11 January 2017